T0196921

AIRBORNE

A Collection of Stories

COMMANDER MARTIN HERZOG

AIRBORNE
A COLLECTION OF STORIES

Copyright © 2019 Commander Martin Herzog.

All rights reserved. No part of this book may be used or reproduced by any means, graphic, electronic, or mechanical, including photocopying, recording, taping or by any information storage retrieval system without the written permission of the author except in the case of brief quotations embodied in critical articles and reviews.

iUniverse books may be ordered through booksellers or by contacting:

iUniverse
1663 Liberty Drive
Bloomington, IN 47403
www.iuniverse.com
1-800-Authors (1-800-288-4677)

Because of the dynamic nature of the Internet, any web addresses or links contained in this book may have changed since publication and may no longer be valid. The views expressed in this work are solely those of the author and do not necessarily reflect the views of the publisher, and the publisher hereby disclaims any responsibility for them.

Any people depicted in stock imagery provided by Getty Images are models, and such images are being used for illustrative purposes only. Certain stock imagery © Getty Images.

ISBN: 978-1-5320-8707-3 (sc)
ISBN: 978-1-5320-8729-5 (e)

Print information available on the last page.

iUniverse rev. date: 11/19/2019

CONTENTS

PREFACE

I am writing this book for my family, in hopes they can enjoy remembering the stories I have been sharing with them for many years. I will be blessed and honored if other readers get enjoyment from the stories as well.

This book is a memoir. Most of the stories are completely factual and first hand, compiled from my thoughts and present-day recollections. However, some of the stories didn't actually happen to me but were related to me. I submit them as second hand stories. Also, I am sure some of the dates and timelines are not exactly correct, as nearly fifty years have transpired since these events occurred and I am depending on my memory, which sadly, is a bit faulty at times.

I am calling this "A Collection of Stories."

Because some of the stories are embarrassing, I have changed names of some of the men about whom the stories are written. Some of the dialog has been recreated. However, most of the names are correct and factual. Most of the embarrassing moments are my own. I "fess up" to my own goof ups.

Memories
   For: Mary
   For: Kevin, Elizabeth and Dominic, MaLisa, Maryel and Jennifer
   For: Justin

Dedicated to my family (listed above) and to all the courageous men listed in memoriam in the Remembering chapter at the end of the book.

CHAPTER 1

COLLEGE YEARS

November 1966 – May 1967

Events in the Navy and Worldwide During This Time

October 26, 1966   *Oriskany* Fire
On 26 October 1966, a magnesium parachute flare exploded hangar bay of *Oriskany*. The resulting fire killed 44 men.

January 27, 1967   Apollo 1
Astronauts Gus Grissom, Edward Higgins White, and Roger Chaffee were killed when fire broke during a launch pad test in their Apollo spacecraft.

February 1, 1967
The first Navy A-7 squadrons reached operational status. They began combat operations over Vietnam in December 1967.

Three Things

Toward the end of the first semester of my senior year at Towson State College, I received a formal letter from the United States government instructing me to report for my pre- induction physical. A pre-induction physical determined one's fitness to serve in the military - to see who was and was not eligible to be drafted. Early on a beautiful, sunny Saturday morning in November 1966, I got in my red 1961 4-door Studebaker Lark and drove to Fort Holabird in Southeast Baltimore to comply with these instructions.

Three things bear mentioning at this point in my story: my car, my school, and my draft status.

My Car

The 1961 Studebaker Lark that I mentioned was the third car I had owned and the only one built in the same decade in which I owned it. My father helped me find all three cars. He was a used car salesman for Al Packer Ford on Belair Road in Baltimore and I trusted him completely to help me find a good car. Often when he sold a car at the dealership, he would take a trade-in which he was allowed to buy at dealer cost. So, he got the Lark for me for a measly $350. What a bargain! Prior to that, I had owned a 1951 Plymouth Cranbrook and a 1953 Chevrolet Belair.

Car #1 - 1951 Plymouth Cranbrook: I purchased this car in 1964 from a friend of my father's, Don Service, for a whopping five dollars. And that's pretty close to what it was worth. Since this car only cost me five dollars, some annoyances were acceptable. After all, this was my first car. No longer did I have to wait for the streetcar or bus to go somewhere. I was a man of means now, a driver.

What annoyances could there be?

1) If I happened to look down while driving, I could see the asphalt of the street passing by under the car - right through the floor boards. They had rusted out so badly that it was precarious just getting in and out of the car. I was instructed to be very careful while getting in and out, so as to not put my foot through the floor.

2

2) Using the brakes was also a bit scary because I was not sure they would always function as intended. Not only that but there was a possibility that my foot might slide off the pedal and right through the previously mentioned rusted floor boards.

3) I had to learn to use a clutch and a stick shift. My girlfriend and I got pretty handy at coordinating our efforts using the stick. I could put my arm around her, she would shift, and I would play the clutch. It took some practice, but we managed to get pretty good at it.

4) I had to carry a supply of oil in the trunk. Every time I stopped for gas, I would have to add at least a quart of oil to bring the level back above the "add oil" line on the dip stick.

5) When I was driving down the road, you could see me coming as billowing smoke marked the trail behind me wherever I went. Sometimes, I wondered whether this Plymouth burned more gas or more oil. But it ran, and it took me from point A to point B as long as point B wasn't up too steep of a hill.

Car #2 – 1953 Chevrolet Belair: My dad found a nicer car for me about six months later. It was a dandy – a two tone (dark green and light green), two door 1953 Chevrolet Belair - a convertible and the top was electric. I could sit in the driver's seat, press a button, and the top would move up and back into the storage boot. All this luxury cost me only $200 and it didn't use nearly as much oil as the Plymouth. I gave the Plymouth to a friend who somehow eventually used it to power a lawn mower.

The Chevy was really great until the accident. I was trying to get home from work during a pretty severe snowstorm in Baltimore, and because of the nearly bald tires that I had, I couldn't get up the hill on Cold Spring Lane. I decided to get a "running start." To do that I would have to turn a corner at a traffic light on Loch Raven Boulevard, left onto Cold Spring Lane, gunning the engine while turning to get the speed necessary to make it up the hill. Sounded like a good plan to me, until I actually tried it. I ended up sliding into a car that was stopped facing the other way on Cold Spring – damaging both cars.

Understandably, the other driver was quite upset at my recklessness and I was out several hundred dollars…more than my car was worth. Time to get another car. So now the Studebaker.

Car #3 – 1961 Studebaker Lark: The Studebaker was my best and newest car of the three. It transported me many miles and lasted nearly a year.

What I never realized was that even though it was relatively new, the odometer indicated over 150,000 miles. Why didn't I look at that before I bought it? It wasn't long before the Lark was acting up, needing more and more oil to survive. It eventually threw a piston rod, completely destroying the engine. Bring on car number four. Well, car number four's story comes later.

My School

After graduating from Baltimore City College (which is actually a high school) in June of 1963, I went to Towson State Teachers College – more properly called Maryland State Teachers College at Towson, but no one called it that. In late 1963, the school's name was officially changed to Towson State College.

Towson State College.

I had a full academic scholarship since my grades in high school were pretty good and I planned on serving the state of Maryland as a teacher upon graduation. My maturity level was not too high at this point, and with my new found collegiate freedom, my work time and my play time got reversed from what they should have been. I ended up skipping many of my freshman classes, so I could play bridge and pinochle in the student center. Those activities

Towson State College

were much more enjoyable than listening to a lecture about something in which I wasn't the least bit interested. I ended up failing freshman English Literature and sophomore United States History. The problem with failing a class, aside from the obvious damage to your grade point average, is that you have to take the course again - double boredom.

I remember one particular moment in my U.S. History class. The professor was an older gentleman, quite a nice person actually, but he had very poor eyesight and had to wear glasses that seemed to be at least half an inch thick. When he looked up at us, he looked like Mister Magoo, with monstrous sized eyes – magnified by those extremely thick glasses.

Now, I obviously wasn't a stellar student (already noted), so on the occasion that I would actually go to class, I would sit in the back row – out of the line of fire – so the professor wouldn't see me and ask me to answer some question on a topic that I hadn't studied. However, this strategy failed me one day. As I was nodding off in the back row, Professor Magoo looked right at me (I don't know if he actually saw me or not) and said, "Yes, in the back row, what do you want?"

As I started to regain consciousness, I realized he was waiting for my response. He said, "Well, what do you want? Do you have a question? If not, put your hand down." Now, my hand was firmly on the desk the entire time. So, I looked around to see if someone else had their hand raised. Nope. It was me. He was fixed on me. Then he said, "Well, then please sit down and put your hand down." By now, I was completely perplexed. What did Professor Magoo want from me? No wonder I was failing. I couldn't understand this guy at all.

By now the entire class was looking in my direction. Many of them were chuckling, I thought, at my misfortune to have been singled out for this harassment. Before long, the chuckling turned into outright laughter and then I noticed that the professor was actually looking over my head. So, I turned around to see what he was looking at. And there on the wall, right behind me was a large picture of the Statue of Liberty. The life-sized Miss Liberty was standing there and had her hand raised. My paranoia turned to relief when the professor finally realized his mistake and went on with his dissertation about some boring aspect of the history of our great country.

After failing U.S. History, I was put on academic probation with a 1.8 grade point average. This was the wake- up call I needed. I realized if I didn't get serious, I would flunk out of college and would most likely be drafted into the Army and sent to Vietnam. Afraid of failing out and losing my scholarship, I came to my senses and finished my remaining two years with much better grades. I graduated in June 1967 with a 2.37 GPA.

My Draft Status

Just before my 18th birthday in November 1963, I had received notification that I should report to the local Selective Service office to register for the draft. The Selective Service System was an independent agency that kept information about male citizens of the United States who might be drafted by the military. All male citizens, ages 18-25 were required by law to register with the Selective Service.

Registered men were classified according to their fitness and availability for military service. The three main categories were:

1-A   Available for unrestricted military service.

2-S   Deferred because of collegiate study (deferred until graduation). Public school teachers were granted this deferment as well in the '60s.

4-F   Not acceptable for military service (because of physical, mental or moral issues).

In 1963, when I first registered, I was attending Towson State College; so I was granted 2-S draft deferment status. During the next few years, I was blissfully unconcerned about serving in the military, since it didn't apply to me. I had more important things to do, like playing pinochle and bridge and failing English Literature and U.S. History. Since I was planning to be a teacher upon graduation, I assumed I would be exempt from the draft for my whole life. My 2-S classification gave me a free ride, or so I thought.

Fort Holabird

Now, let's rejoin the story on that beautiful, sunny Saturday morning three years later in November 1966 at Fort Holabird.

After I arrived and parked my car, I went to the building where the pre-induction physicals were being held. There was a rather long line of young men standing outside the entrance. I joined them. While we were waiting, we discussed what we had heard about the physical and mental testing that awaited us. One of the guys in line told us that he was going to try to fail – to get a 4-F classification.

He demonstrated how he was going to talk, lisping and using words like "Sweetie" and "Sugar," when he referred to me or other men. Then he showed us the top of his underwear. He was wearing ladies' panties. He was pretending to be homosexual. In those days, homosexuals were not permitted to serve in the Armed Forces. He told us he wasn't homosexual, but wanted the Army to think that he was, so he would be unacceptable to them. I began wondering how that was going to work out for him once we got inside.

He also told us if we didn't want to pass, we could easily fail the written test. Failing tests was something I was already pretty good at, but later when we were actually taking the written test, the sergeant administering it said, "If any of you fail this test, you will actually pass, because if you're smart enough to know the wrong answers, then you are obviously smart enough to know the right answers." I couldn't quite figure out this logic. "Is this the way the Army works?" I wondered. "I must have a lot to learn." I decided to be honest and try to do my best on the test, in spite of what the "panty-guy" told me.

The building we were about to enter seemed like a hangar without airplanes. It was big, tall, and wide. After getting into it, we were ushered into a large room, where we took what the Sergeant called "The Intelligence Test." As I began the test, I realized that a junior high school student could pass it. Certainly, a college student had the "intelligence" to pass it.

When the testing time was over, we left the room and were led to a yellow line on the cement floor. We were told to go from station to station following the yellow line, stopping at each station for a part of our examination.

So, that's what we did. At one station, someone listened to our breathing; at another, someone took blood pressures, then an ear examination and so on. They were poking and prodding us in various places until the yellow line led us to a closed door with a sign on it that said "WAIT HERE."

After waiting fifteen minutes or so, the door opened, and another sergeant told us to come in. By now, there were about 20 of us waiting outside the door.

Once inside the room, the single yellow line became two yellow lines. The sergeant told us to separate into two equal groups, one group on each line. He had us turn so that we all were facing the same direction, two lines with ten guys each, lined up side by side. The door was closed, and we were told to strip down to our under shorts. So, that's what we did.

Then a man wearing a white lab coat came in carrying a stethoscope and a flashlight. We were told that he was a doctor, but I was never completely convinced about that. The sergeant turned off the lights and told us to open our mouths wide as the doctor came by. The doctor went down each row and held the flashlight high and close to our mouths while he peered down our throats, or at our teeth, tongue or tonsils. He never told us what he was looking for. It was all a great mystery.

He never said anything or wrote anything down. Then the sergeant said that the doctor was going to examine our eyes. He went through the same routine, only more quickly. It was like he was just checking to see if we, in fact, had eyes.

He walked down each row, shining the light in our faces, not stopping in front of any of us and again, not saying anything or writing anything down.

The next part of this "examination" was absolutely astounding to me. The sergeant told us to all drop our shorts, bend over and "spread our cheeks". Many of the guys had never heard their buttocks referred to as "cheeks" and needed clarification from the sergeant, which he provided, embellished with some profanity that everyone understood. So, there we were, twenty guys in two lines, bent over, cheeks spread and the doctor with his flashlight. It must have been a sight to see.

Once again, the doc went down each row, quickly examining our behinds. He stopped behind one of the guys, telling the sergeant something that I couldn't hear. This was followed by the sergeant yelling at this young man who probably weighed 300-350 pounds. He was a big fellow and I surmised that he must have had big "cheeks" because the sergeant said, "The doctor can't see. You need to spread your cheeks wider." The big boy said, "I'm a-spreadin' 'em." Sarge said, "No, you aren't! Here, look at this guy next to you. See how he's doing it?" Big Boy straightened up and looked at the guy on his left and said, "Ahhh. Now I get it." He bent over and reassumed the spreading position with his new directions. The doc seemed satisfied, nodded and continued down the row examining every young man's posterior parts.

After that indignity, he left the room. We were told to dress and go out the door that said "OUT." By this time, I had formed the opinion that the Army didn't waste money putting eloquent words on signage. I was getting an education about the military. While I was dressing, I gave some thought to how in the world anyone could fail this kind of physical examination.

I couldn't help but wonder what happened to the Panty- Guy. Did he make it past the psychiatrist station? What did the rear end doc think of him with his women's underwear? How about the other guys in the room? Did he even make it to the exam room? I never found out because I never saw him again.

Soon, the pre-induction physical was over, and I was driving my Studebaker home – back to sanity and normal civilian life.

Joining the Navy

In early January of 1967, I received another letter from the Selective Service. As I opened it, I was hoping that it wasn't going to tell me to come back to Fort Holabird for more testing. Did I fail the physical? No. That was impossible!

The letter had my new draft card, with my updated draft classification based upon the results of the pre-induction physical. I was 1-A. Oh no! That meant I would be drafted. There was no lottery in those days. Everyone who was classified 1-A planned on two years in the Army. Now I started to get scared. I didn't want to be in the Army. I didn't want to go to Vietnam and get shot at. What was going on? I was supposed to be deferred, at least until graduation, and that wouldn't be until June. After that I was supposed to be deferred as a school teacher.

I paid a visit to my local draft board to appeal the re- classification. The man at the main desk said that an appeal would do me no good. Schoolteacher deferments had been curtailed. I would be able to complete my education but could be in the Army the day after graduation.

I started working on an amazingly simple strategy that would spare me from having to join the Army. I would join the Navy. In the Navy, you were on a ship. You were safe. No one was shooting at you. Now, I could do that. But I was concerned that the Army would get me before I had a chance to finish college and before I could enlist in the Navy.

So, in February 1967, I went to the Navy Building in Washington, D.C. to see what my options in the Navy might be. After I had parked my Studebaker, I headed for the main ADMIN building. I was a math major and I knew that the shortest distance between two points is a straight line. The straight line between my car and the front door of the ADMIN building happened to pass over a grassy area, which I ignorantly walked through, ignoring the sign, "STAY OFF THE GRASS."

Almost immediately, a guy with a blue uniform and a sailor cap yelled at me, "Keep off the *%^&* grass! Where the *%^&* do you think you are going?" It must have been this guy's job to keep the grass healthy and to yell at people who tried to walk on it. He was really good at his work. He had a way with spoken English that I had never heard before. I jumped about a foot in the air and was out of the grass without another foot touching it. I started wondering if joining the Navy was really such a good idea.

Well, I was already at the ADMIN building, so I thought I would take the long way around the grassy area to the front door and see what awaited me inside. When I got inside, there was a round elevated desk with another Navy man behind it.

He was a bit older and had a whole lot of ribbons on his chest and a lot of gold stripes on the arm of his uniform. He seemed pleasant enough and asked me if he could help me.

I told him that I was a senior at Towson State College, graduating in June, and wanted to become an officer in the Navy. He seemed pleased to hear that and pulled out a rather large notebook and thumbed through it. Then, he said, "Tsk, tsk, tsk. There isn't an opening in Officer Candidate School for over a year." Oh, no. If I had to wait for an entire year, the Army would certainly draft me. I couldn't wait that long. I realized that I wasn't the only one who was avoiding service in the Army.

Dejected, I turned to leave, wondering what I could do to keep from being drafted into the Army. The man behind the desk was a C.P.O. (Chief Petty Officer). "ARMS" was written on a name tag over his right chest pocket. As I was heading out the door, Chief Arms called me. "Young man, would you be willing to consider pilot training? I have openings in Aviation Officer Candidate School, if you are qualified." Without a moment's hesitation, I said "Yes," not thinking about the fact that pilots in Vietnam, even Navy pilots, get shot at just like the Army guys.

Chief Arms wrote my name in the notebook and gave me some forms to fill out. When they were completed, he told me to report to Naval Air Facility (N.A.F.) Washington in April to begin my evaluation – to see if I was physically and aeronautically qualified to be a pilot in the Navy.

On a Saturday in early May (my Navy exam date had been changed from April to May), I drove to Andrews Air Force Base, which is where N.A.F. Washington, D.C. is located. At the front gate, the guard directed me to the building where the testing was to occur. I headed for the building, not knowing what to expect. My last physical at Fort Holabird was still fresh in my memory.

However, this series of tests was much more serious. The written test took several hours and was very comprehensive. The physical exam was much more thorough than any physical I had ever had. The last item on the physical exam check list was the eye test. When I got into Eye Exam Room #1, I looked around for the doctor's flashlight. I was relieved to see that although he did look into my eyes with a light, it wasn't a foot-long flashlight like the one the doctor at Fort Holabird had used. I knew this test was important if I was to be a pilot.

When it was time to read the eye chart, I could only manage to read the line that qualified me as 20/25. I needed to be 20/20. Since I had passed everything so far, the doctor suggested that I retake the eye exam the following Saturday. I should rest my eyes, get plenty of sleep and not do a lot of intense reading. I was fine with that. Reading was not my forte.

I came back the next Saturday, after obeying the doctor's orders. He remembered me and said we were going to use Eye Exam Room #2. "Sometimes people do better in this room than in Exam Room #1," he said. We went in and I passed! 20/20!

The doc told me I could take the oath of office the same afternoon if I wanted to. There were a number of other prospective aviators enlisting at 1 P.M. (1300 – Navy time). I thought I might be pressing my luck with the draft if I waited, so I decided to sign up as soon as possible, before my luck ran out and the Army grabbed me. So, I joined this group and on May 11, 1967 I was sworn in and became a Navy man.

As I drove home to Baltimore, I had a number of emotions running through me…happiness, anxiety, curiosity, fear of the unknown, but primarily relief that the course of action before me didn't include the Army or rice paddies in Vietnam.

When I got home, there was another government letter waiting for me, from the Department of the Army. "Greetings," it said and went on the say that I would be inducted into the Army at some date in July or August 1967.

"They got me!" I thought, "After all of this work, am I going to be inducted into the Army? This is horrible!" I called N.A.F. Washington right away and actually spoke to the officer who swore me in. He chuckled at my distress and told me, "Don't worry about that letter. As a matter of fact, you can keep it as a souvenir or burn it if you like. You will not be drafted. You're in the Navy now."

I completed my undergraduate degree and graduated from Towson State College four weeks later. Three and a half months after that I began my Naval career with a trip to Pensacola, Florida.

CHAPTER 2

Aviation Officer Candidate School – A.O.C.S.

October 1967 - January 1968

Events in the Navy During This Time

October 26, 1967

U.S. Navy pilot John McCain was shot down over North Vietnam and was captured.

Pensacola, Florida

The first stop or duty station in my Navy career was in Pensacola. On October 2, 1967, I flew American Airlines into Pensacola International Airport, rented a car, and drove right to Pensacola Beach. I parked and walked to the boardwalk to look at the beautiful, blue Gulf of Mexico. The water was amazingly clear and blue, so I took my shoes off and walked on the

Pensacola Beach

beach. I was impressed again: this time with how clean the sand was. It actually squeaked when you walked on it. Imagine that.

I met a guy on the boardwalk who asked me if I was reporting to Aviation Officer Candidate School (A.O.C.S.) I had no idea what gave him that impression. I told him "Yes," and he gave me some unsolicited advice. "I hope you're not planning on reporting today. You don't want to report until you have to. Certainly not a whole day early." I didn't tell him but I was, in fact, planning to report that day. I had nothing else to do. But I took his warning to heart and spent the night in a local hotel on Palafox Avenue and reported the next day.

Gulf of Mexico

Indoc Battalion

The next afternoon, after returning my rented car, I got a taxi to take me to the base: Naval Air Station, Pensacola. I was dropped off at Building 100, later to be known as "Splinterville" or "Indoc." There were three guys, about my age, dressed in khakis standing on the steps as I exited the cab in front of my new home. One of them came down to me and helped me with my suitcase. He had quite a few bars on his collar. I naturally thought, "He must be important." He asked me, "Are you reporting to A.O.C.S?" He walked me up the steps, took a copy of my orders, and told me to put my suitcase over in the corner. He gestured to a stack of suitcases left by other reporting candidates. "What do you want to fly? Jets?" I hadn't given that question much thought, but jets sounded cool. So, casually, I said "Yeah."

After he took my orders and I got inside the building, his demeanor changed. He wasn't as friendly as before. He said, "The first word out of your mouth, any time you speak is 'sir'. Now, try it." I got the message. "Sir" came out of my mouth. He noticed my shirt wasn't buttoned up all the way. He told me to button every button, otherwise the buttons weren't doing their job. "Yes Sir." Next, he showed me how to stand at attention. Heels together, feet at a 90-degree angle, chest out, stomach in, no looking around, shoulders back, chin straight, eyes front. "No looking around!" "Get your shoulders back!" "Keep your heels together!" "No moving!" he shouted. Didn't this guy have anything else to do? I wondered, "Why does he have to yell? I can hear. Why was he harassing me? What have I done?"

All the while this guy with the bars was laying into me, other candidates were reporting and getting the same treatment from other guys dressed in khakis. Then, we got some relief when a candidate came in carrying a surfboard. He drew a lot of attention and the rest of us got a short reprieve. He was immediately dubbed "Surfer Joe."

After delivering his surfboard to the pile of suitcases, he was told to demonstrate how to catch a wave. He was taken over to the steps and told to "Hang ten." On a surfboard, hanging ten means to have your ten toes over the front edge of the board while surfing. He had to hang ten on the steps for about 10-15 minutes. The khaki guys got a big kick out of this. But pretty soon the novelty wore off and they were back to the rest of us.

This harassing activity went on for over an hour before those of us who had been there the longest were directed to our bunk rooms, given a blanket, pillow and linens, and told to prepare our "racks." We were starting to learn some of the Navy lingo. A "rack" was a bed. The day seemed like utter chaos to me, but no one was asking me what I thought. The only question that I was asked was, "Do you want to D.O.R.?" More Navy lingo: Drop On Request, or in English – quit. Did I want to quit? What a question! I just got here. The khaki guys must have gotten some sort of award if we D.O.R.ed because they kept on asking us if we wanted to do it.

We were instructed to get out of our "raggedy civilian clothes" and put on a poopy suit and boondockers. A poopy suit looked somewhat like a flight suit except it was made of cotton and was heavier. It was green and had about 20 buttons down the front. We were to button every single one of them. Boondockers were the black boots that we wore. They came up to the bottom of our calves and had about 15 eyelets through which the boot laces had to be strung in a precise manner...outer lace over the inner lace, all the way from the lowest eyelet to the top eyelet.

The first 10 days of A.O.C.S. were spent in Splinterville, in Indoc Battalion. Boy, was I getting an indoctrination! My first day in the Navy, mercifully, came to a close at 10:00 PM or 2200. We were told that when "Taps" was played we were to be in our racks and there would be no noise until Reveille. The Khaki guys told us that if we thought the first day was rough, just wait until tomorrow when the D.I. got a hold of us. "What is a D.I.?" I wondered.

At 4:30 AM, we heard a scratchy sound coming through the speakers in the hallway. It was a record player. Then it played "Reveille", followed by someone yelling in the hallway. Immediately awake, I thought, "What? It's still night time. It's not morning yet. It's still dark outside!" Then more yelling, "Get up! Get your scummy bodies dressed and out the back door. Go! Now! Out! Out! Out!" I never knew how fast I could dress before. I had my poopy suit on and buttoned in a flash. We ran out the back door to a parking lot where there was even more yelling. "Line up, girls. Shoulder to shoulder. No noise. Get those buttons buttoned! Where do you think you are? at the Y.W.C.A.?"

Then, I saw him. The D.I. The previous night, I had found out that D.I. stood for Drill Instructor, a Marine non- commissioned officer, generally a gunnery sergeant or a staff sergeant. He stood there dressed in a khaki uniform with a "Smokey the Bear" hat. The dreaded D.I., Sergeant Grelish was the man we would have to reckon with for the next ten days. When we were all lined up to his satisfaction, he told us "Now, ladies. I am Gunnery Sergeant Grelish. It is my job to make you scumbags into a platoon. After looking at you, I don't see how that is going to be possible. Now we are going to march down to the P.T. area and wake your nasty bodies up with some pushups. And if you don't like it, you can D.O.R." A—ten—hut! Ri--eat Face! Fo—ward March!" There it was again ... D.O.R. Do they all want us to quit? If we quit, who would they have to yell at?

The next day, we went to a classroom on the second floor of Splinterville. Sergeant Grelish came in and said, "The Navy must think that you girls are all heroes because I'm going to give you your first medal.

18

Maybe you earned this because you didn't D.O.R. on the first day."
National Defense Medals and ribbons were distributed to all of us. No
fanfare. This "award" was given to everyone who was in the armed forces
during that period of time. "You will put this medal away and I don't want
to see it again until you have a dress blues or dress whites inspection."

A few days later, we got measured for our Navy black shoes. All
of us were lined up outside the second-floor classroom waiting to be
measured. We were told that after we were measured, we were to "hustle
our butts out to the parking lot behind the building." This parking lot
was known as the Grinder. Standing in line meant that your toe was
touching the heel of the guy in front of you. The D.I.s got a big kick
out of that. "I want you to get reeeeal friendly with the man in front of
you and the one behind you. Get to know each other. Are you smiling?
I saw you smiling. You better not be smiling."

Finally, it was my turn to be measured. I stepped on the shoe size
apparatus and it was done. The D.I. said, "What are you waiting for? Get
out of here!" I got my boondockers on while hopping on one foot down
the stairs. Then I began to run through an open area in the building below
the classroom, and then down the hallway towards the Grinder. "Hey! You!
Hit it!" Oh No. Now what? I stopped on a dime and braced up at
attention against the left wall (bulkhead) and waited. Out of the corner
of eye – I had already learned that you never turned your head – I saw
a khaki uniform approaching. It was another D.I. They were everywhere!
I found out later that his name was Staff Sergeant White.

He was a short guy but wide at the
shoulders. He grabbed my poopy suit
about halfway between my navel and my
neck and lifted me nearly off the ground. I
was on my toes. "Do you know what you
just did?" "No Sir," I shouted. By now,
we had learned to shout out anything
communicated to a D.I. "Were they all
hard of hearing?" I wondered. "You just
went through God's Country." I had no
idea what he was talking about. "You will

"God's Country"
Quarterdeck

never go through God's Country again, Will you?" -- No argument from me. "NO SIR!" was the obvious reply. "Get going!" "YES SIR!" "Go! Go! Go! Go!" He let me go and I took off at full speed for the parking lot.

I found out later that in the open space under the second floor classroom were four three-foot-high poles surrounding several flags. That area was called the quarterdeck. Sergeant White was referring to that area as God's Country. Needless to say, I avoided him and that area for the rest of the time I was in Indoc.

Marching

Part of our military education was marching as a unit, a platoon. I couldn't quite understand why a pilot would need to march but, by now, I knew better than to ask "why." We must not have been very good at it because Sergeant Grelish kept telling us we were diddlely-bopping, not marching. Since I was one of the taller candidates, I could see what he meant because I was usually at the rear of the column. There would be about 60 of us in rows of four. If we were all marching in step, it was a wonderful sight to see ... our heads would rise and fall simultaneously. But if someone was the least bit out of step with the rest of us, his head would be up while the rest were down. Diddlely-bopping.

If we were marching in step, the D.I. would call cadences in a sing-song fashion. "Left .. Left .. and your left, right, left."

I can still hear him singing that out. It was comforting to hear him singing cadence because you knew he was at least somewhat pleased. Sometimes he would sing something that we were supposed to sing back to him while we're marching.

D.I.:	"I don't know but it's been said." (singing)
Platoon:	"I don't know but it's been said." (singing)
D.I.:	"Air Force wings are made of lead"
Platoon:	"Air Force wings are made of lead"
D.I.:	"I don't know but I've been told."
Platoon:	"I don't know but I've been told."

D.I.:   "Navy wings are made of gold."
Platoon: "Navy wings are made of gold."

When the D.I. was happy, all was well in our world, but diddlely-bopping did not make the D.I. happy. If he was not pleased, our marching session would terminate and we would end up in "The Playpen." That was an area between two wings of Splinterville where no grass grew. It was only loose sand and dirt. When you marched or walked in it for a while, a cloud of dust would rise about 6 feet in the air, making it hard to even breathe.

The command we would hear if things were going well would be "Column left … March!" But when we were diddlely- bopping, the singing cadence would stop and we'd hear "You're diddlely-bopping! Get in step!" If we didn't correct matters very quickly, we would hear. "All right, girls. Turn left." We knew something was wrong and we were in trouble.

Then we would be in the Playpen. The D.I. would get up on a podium… no dust up there? He must have done this before. Did he know we were coming in here today? "Everyone – Down for push-ups! Assume the position." Then the torture would begin. The D.I. would yell "Down!" We would go down and up, shouting "One, sir!" when we got back to the starting position. "Down" – "Two, sir!" "Down" – "Three, sir!" and so on. The dust level began to rise and … thicken.

When he got tired of push-ups, we would do what we called "Bellies." Sergeant Grelish would yell, "On your bellies!" We were expected to flop down on the ground smacking our bellies to the dirt. Then "On your backs!" Now we were expected to launch ourselves into the air and turn over, landing on our backs. "On your bellies." Another launch and landing. This could go on for five minutes – completely exhausting all of us, except the D.I. He said, "I could do this for hours." Then after a while, a second chance.

"Are you ready to try marching again?" "YES SIR"
"No diddlely-bopping this time?" "NO SIR"
"Because if you do, you know where you'll end up?"
"YES SIR"
"All right! Get back in formation! Now!!!"

We were tired and really dirty. Our faces were completely black except for where sweat had made streaks through the dirt. But we managed to hustle it back to the Grinder, line up, start marching again. Before long, Sergeant Grelish was singing again. Thank goodness. I can't wait to get a shower. How long before Taps?

Inspections

We had formal inspections nearly every day. R.L.P.s were major evolutions. R.L.P. stands for Room, Locker and Personnel Inspection. It would take us an hour or longer to get ready for these inspections. There were quite a few things on our inspection checklist.

1) Our room: Each room had a room captain. That assignment rotated among the candidates in the room. The room captain was responsible for the room's overall appearance. Actually, we were all responsible, but the room captain was the one who would get yelled at for an untidy room. He also had to give the "report" when the D.I. showed up at the door. The D.I. would slam the side of the door three times with the palm of his hand and then enter. This was called "Pounding the Pine." After he pounded the pine, the room captain was to sound off: "Sir! Aviation Officer Candidate Hodges reports room 7 ready for Room, Locker and Personnel Inspection."

2) Our tables: Our room had 3 tables. A table was to be shared by two candidates. There were six of us in room 7. On each half of the table a candidate would put several pairs of highly shined shoes or boondockers, shined belt buckles and belts with the tips polished, and other various items that the D.I.s wanted on the table for that inspection. After just a few days, we figured out that you don't wear your inspection items. You keep them protected from inspection to inspection, so they stay in good condition.

3) Our dressers: Top drawer was for undershirts that were folded in perfect 6 inch by 6-inch squares with the neck at the top

precisely in the middle. Underpants the same way. Everyone was issued boxers - no whitey tighties for us. Socks had their prescribed place, and folding directions and so forth for all of our Naval issue.

4) Our closets: They were called "lockers" - Two men to a locker. They housed all of our hanging clothes: dress uniforms, overcoats, jackets, all evenly spaced exactly one inch from hanger to hanger.

5) Our uniform: Each inspection would highlight a different Naval uniform. We would be wearing it and it had better be neat and properly worn.

When the hour came for the inspection, two or three D.I.s would examine one room at a time while the rest of us agonized, waiting for our turn. When they came to our room, one of them pounded the pine, the room captain reported, and then chaos ensued. They were never happy with anything. They would open the window and just about everything in our room would be thrown outside on the grass: boots, belts, underwear … everything.

While this was happening, they asked us questions like, "Who is the Secretary of State?" "Who is the Third Battalion Officer? "Who is the President of the United States?" Our answer would be "Sir! The President of the United States is the Honorable Lyndon B. Johnson!" – Shouted, of course. Nothing was ever spoken in a normal voice.

One of my roommates was asked, "Who is the Vice President of the United States?" He said, "Sir! (pause) Sir! (pause) The Vice President of the United States is the Honorable (pause and then somewhat triumphantly) Humphrey!" Uh oh – He didn't say "Hubert Humphrey." I could tell that he could not recollect the Vice President's first name. The D.I. was all over him. "Humphrey? Humphrey? Humphrey who? Humphrey Bogart? I didn't know he was the vice president." Feeling proud of himself, the D.I. moved on to another moment of humiliation, by pulling my roommate's shirt out of his trousers, telling him his "gig line" wasn't straight. A gig-line is the line that your shirt buttons make with your trouser zipper. That line was supposed to be perfectly straight and vertical. While this was happening, the rest of us were being harassed by the other D.I.s. No one ever really passed these inspections, but the Sergeants seemed to enjoy them immensely.

My questions that day were less straight-forward. "Candidate Herzog, do you like me?" I immediately realized that there was no good answer to that question. If I said "Yes Sir" he would accuse me of being homosexual, which was totally unacceptable in those days. If I said "No Sir" then he would want to know why. So, I said, "Sir, I don't understand the question that you are asking me." Wrong Answer! Did I just refer to the D.I. as you? That was not allowed. I should have said "Sir, I don't understand the question that the Drill Instructor asked me." So, with my mistake, the D.I. was now saying "You? Ewe? Ewe? Are you calling me a female goat?" Now I was in real trouble. There was no way out so I tried to make amends. "NO SIR. This candidate was not referring to the Drill Instructor as a female goat." Fortunately, something else caught his eye and the discussion was over for the moment. Whew!

Hodges in the closet

The next R.L.P., two days later, was rather eventful. The D.I.s started several rooms away from ours. We were standing at attention by our racks, one at the head and one at the foot of each rack. We were supposed to stand at attention during the entire inspection, even while the D.I.s were in a different room. Today, it was Candidate Hodges's turn to be room captain. We felt like we were as prepared as we could be, but continued looking around for any obvious thing that we could quickly and covertly fix before the sergeants came. The table looked good, everything spaced properly. Our racks looked good, no visible wrinkles. The lockers looked good and the locker doors were opened 12 inches as they were supposed to be.

Then, to our horror, a ball of dust and hair, looking something like a two-inch tumbleweed rolled in the door from the hallway. These balls were called "ghost turds." I don't know who came up that name but it stuck and there was one rolling right into the middle of our room. If the D.I.s saw it, we would be in deep trouble. Hodges whispered to us, "Somebody get it." – the answer whispered back "You're the room captain. You get it." Hodges started to creep toward the tumbleweed and it started rolling again. It rolled and Hodges, leaning over behind it, followed it right into our closet.

Hodges bumped the closet door and it closed behind him, with him on the inside. Wouldn't you know? That was the exact moment Sergeant Grelish pounded our pine.

Hodges was the room captain and he was in the closet. The sergeant wasn't a math major but he could count to six and there were only five of us visible in the room. Then Hodges sounded off with his report as room captain from inside the closet. It was muffled, but everyone knew what it was. "SIR, Aviation … …odges, reports …. seven ready for …… and person…. inspection"

Sergeant Grelish tilted his head to the side and looked around. He looked at each of us, one at a time, wondering who the ventriloquist was. "Where is the room captain?" No answer. He came over to me. "Who is the room captain?" No use being deceptive. That would only get us in more trouble. We were already wondering what was going to happen to us. "SIR, the room captain is Aviation Officer Candidate Hodges."

Sergeant Grelish: "Candidate Hodges – Sound off!"

And from the closet…"SIR! Aviation Officer Candidate Hodges is here, SIR." The sergeant slowly walked over to the closet door and noticed that it was closed. It should have been open. He put his hand on the knob and whipped it open! There was Hodges, at attention, one inch away from where the door was a moment ago. The sergeant looked at him – up and down. Oh boy! What's going to happen now? Then Hodges, still standing at a perfect attention, said "Going up, Sir?"

The other two D.I.s, who were watching this whole scene with intense curiosity, were smiling. One of them covered his mouth. I couldn't help looking at Sergeant Grelish out of the corner of my eye. His lip was quivering. He looked around. It looked like he wanted to laugh, but there was no way he was going to let us see that. He and the other two D.I.s left the room and walked down the hallway to their office without saying a word to anybody. We didn't hear from them for about fifteen minutes. When they came back to finish the R.L.P. inspection, they picked up with room 8, completely bypassing us. My guess was that they couldn't come back into our room without bursting out laughing. That was the first inspection that we ever passed. Our shoes were still on the table and nothing went out the window. Hodges was still in the closet, smiling.

A New Home

After the ten days of Indoc, we were told to pack our duffel bags and get out to the grinder. We were going to our new home and were going to meet our new Drill Instructor. Out on the grinder, in formation with our packs, we set off on a six-block walk to the Battalion Three Barracks. Once there, we were alphabetically divided into two groups of about thirty candidates and given a class number. My group was 38-67 Echo. The other group was 38-67 Foxtrot. Our new Drill Instructor was Sergeant Washington. He must have been from the South. He had a Southern accent and referred to us as "Hummeroos." I never quite understood what a hummeroo was, but it didn't seem to be too bad, maybe like a kangaroo or a buckaroo. A few weeks later, we even made a class banner with "Washington's Hummeroos" on it.

Washington's Hummeroos

There were three aspects to the next 9 weeks of our training: Academics, Physical Fitness and Military.

1) Academics: We went to the education building every day for: Naval Justice, Effective Communication, Navigation, Naval Orientation, Naval History, and Naval Leadership.

2) Physical Fitness: Something every day - Obstacle Course, Cross Country Course, and Swimming.
3) Military: Inspections, Watch Standing, Marching, and Bearing.

We wore name tags that were colored red, white, yellow or black:

1) Yellow if you excelled in one of the three areas (Academics, Military, Physical) during the previous week.
2) Red if you excelled in two.
3) White if you excelled in all three.
4) Black if you didn't excel in any of the three.

Candidates who had a white name tag were rare and were called "Snowflakes." Name tags were updated weekly. I had a red one for one week (physical fitness and academics – I had a few lucky tests.), but most of the time I had a yellow one for physical fitness.

Watch standing consisted of standing the "Mate of the Deck" watch, which entailed sitting behind a large desk, answering the phone and doing errands for the Drill Instructor. His office was one room away. I was standing the watch one day, when he loudly said, "M O D !!!" That was me. M.O.D. – Mate of the Deck. I sprang from my seat and went to his office, pounded his pine three times, and waited for permission to enter his office. He simply said, "ENTER," and told me what he wanted. "Get me a cup of Joe." "YES SIR!" Not knowing what Joe was, I raced from the room to find out. Opening the M.O.D. notebook, I found out that Joe was coffee and Sergeant Washington liked his with a "touch" of cream.

Surprisingly, I did reasonably well with my academics, except, I failed Naval History and had to repeat it. Does that sound familiar? History – my nemesis. Physical fitness was my strong suit. I was one of the seven best cross-country runners in my class. (The top seven in each class of 60 were called "rabbits"). I also did pretty well with the Obstacle Course (O-Course). So, I was able to get an "Excel" in Physical Fitness nearly every week. Academics and Military, not so much.

Another Encounter with Sergeant White

We were always learning – new things every day. My encounter with Sergeant White in Indoc Battalion taught me several things. One thing was that I would avoid him in the future. But sometimes circumstances don't allow to you to follow your own plans and desires. A few weeks after our original encounter, we crossed paths again. He taught me a seemingly simple lesson that I use to this day.

Our battalion had daily personnel inspections – each morning in fact. A D.I. would walk up and down each row of candidates standing at attention, inspecting our uniforms, shoes and personal grooming. Before reporting for inspection each morning, we would shower, shave and put on a fresh, clean, highly starched khaki uniform with anchor insignia on each collar and a fore and aft cap. We had a limited amount of time to get this all done. My abbreviated shaving technique was a set of quick swipes with my razor down on each cheek and then a set of swipes on both sides of my neck and that was it.

One morning Sergeant White was our inspecting D.I. After looking at the candidates to my right, he stopped in front of me and looked at my neck. Then he asked me "May I touch you"? Now, what was I going to say? No? Naturally I gave him permission. He lightly rubbed his index finger sideways and then upwards on my neck, feeling my shave. Then he explained to me, very nicely, that beards often grow in different directions. Part of your beard might grow to the left and another part might grow downward. Sometimes a beard will grow in a swirl. I should learn which way different areas of my beard grow and shave opposite that direction to get the closest possible shave. He explained to me that the beard on the left side of my neck grew to the right and the beard on my right side grew to the left - sideways. I took this newly acquired revelation to heart and adjusted my shaving technique, resulting in much closer shaves.

More Marching

Our class became known as good marchers. I think the credit for that goes to the D.I. He taught us to use our heels to make a unified, synchronized noise while we were marching. We could all hear it and it helped to keep us together. No more diddlely-bopping for us. Every Friday when a class of Aviation Candidate Officers was commissioned, there was a parade with marching competition between the three battalions. We (Batt Three) regularly won this competition. The heel thing worked very well for us, except by the end of the nine weeks, we all needed some shoe/boot repair.

We learned to follow all of the marching commands:

"Fo—ward March" "To the rear – March"
"Column right (left) – March"
"By the right (left) Flank – March"
"Halt – One Two"

All of these commands had to be given on the proper foot, while we were marching, or there would be horrible results, such as guys marching into each other or turning before they were supposed to. No problem with that though, since the D.I. was giving all the commands.

Aviation Officer Candidates

There were a few commands that we learned that I don't think are in the book. The two that come to mind are "Hit it!" and "Queen Anne's Salute."

"Hit it" was really cool. While we were marching, the D.I. would command, "Hit It!" while we were on our left foot and on the next left, we would stomp really hard with our heel, trying to make as big of a unified stomp as we could.

The Drill Instructors were very playful and seemed to enjoy playing tricks on each other and on us. Queen Anne's Salute was more or less a joke to be played on someone we were marching past, generally another D.I. Commands to be given (if the one being "honored" was on the right) were:

> "Halt – one two"
> "Right Face"
> "Queen Anne's -- Salute"
> "Ready – To"
> "Left Face"
> "Fo—ward March"

On the command "Queen Anne's Salute" the whole company was supposed to raise their right hand with the middle finger extended and leave it there until command "Ready To" was given. Then we were supposed to snap our hands down to our side like we were completing a salute.

We never knew exactly who Queen Anne was or why she had this kind of salute named after her, but Sergeant Washington really enjoyed saluting the other D.I.s

Rifle Inspections

Marching seemed to be pretty easy for us after a while, but then we were issued inoperative M-1 rifles to march with. It was like starting all over. We had to learn new commands:

> "Order Arms"
> "Port Arms"
> "Right (left) Shoulder Arms"
> "Parade Rest"
> "Present Arms"
> "Inspection Arms"

Having rifles gave the D.I.s another reason to have an inspection. We were supposed to clean our rifles regularly. However, no matter how hard we tried, the Drill Instructor could always find something amiss. "There's a smudge on your rifle butt." "There's oil in the barrel." "Your gun sight is dirty." If we didn't pass the inspection, and we rarely did, we would have to sleep with our rifles. They had to be next to us in our racks all night. Sergeant Washington gave each of our rifles a name. Mine was named Betty-Lou. Others were Mary- Jo, Willie-Mae, Ellen-Margaret and so forth.

Just before Taps, on the evening after our rifle inspection, Sergeant Washington got on the speaker from his office and broadcasted to our bunk room: "Is Mary-Jo nice and comfortable?" "Betty-Lou, are you warm?" He was having some fun. We could tell it was all good natured. He never seemed angry. But by the same token, we knew we really did have to sleep with our rifles.

During one inspection, Sergeant Washington was examining our shaves. Were they close enough? Could he see any beard at all? While doing that, he would ask the same kind of questions we were used to: "Who is the Secretary of the Navy?" "Who is the Speaker of the House?" I wondered if Sergeant Washington actually knew these answers himself and was tempted to give some fictitious name in reply, but I never had the courage to do that.

As the sergeant was getting a reply to one of his questions from Candidate Keets, he said, "Whew. You have got some really bad breath." Then he grabbed the candidate, standing at attention next to him, and put him nose to nose with Keets and asked him, "Smell that. Doesn't he have bad breath?" "YES SIR" "Get back in line. Who told you to get out of formation?" The next day, the unfortunate Candidate Keets had to carry a giant bottle of Scope everywhere he went and on command, he had to gargle with it.

"Present -- Scope"	The bottle produced and held chest high at attention.
"Cap – re--move"	Scope cap removed, being careful not to drop it. That would lead to a whole new set of consequences.

"Ready - Swig"	Bottle brought up to the mouth and swig taken.
"Gargle – Huh"	Head back and gargle making gargling noises.
"Ready - To"	Head forward, spit out the used mouthwash. Return to attention saying "Ahhhhhh."

This was always done outdoors on the grass. Whenever one of Sergeant Washington's friends came by, this group of commands would be demonstrated for them. "Candidate Keets, you better not spit any of that on my friend."

Home for Christmas

After the nine weeks at Third Battalion, we were given our Candidate Officer assignments. We were separated into three groups to "lead" each of the three battalions during our last week in A.O.C.S. We didn't really lead them. That fell to the D.I.s and the Company Officers, but we had lesser leadership roles.

Shortly after getting our assignments, we were sent on Christmas leave for 10 days. I hastily packed my bags and hopped a plane for Baltimore, looking forward to some "down time."

At home, I ran into some of my old band buddies. We played music together in a rock band while I was in college. I went with them to a gig they were playing at a club in Baltimore. The people at the club were a bit older than the ones I was used to playing for. After the first set, one of my friends said, "Hey, do you want to meet John Mackey?" He was a tight end for the Baltimore Colts. Everyone in Baltimore knew who he was. I said, "You bet. Where is he?" My friend said "Over there." and pointed to a small crowd with one head higher than all the others. The books had him at 6'2" and 224 pounds. These days that seems small, but back then he was BIG. I think he was bigger than 6'2" - 224. I got to shake his hand and it was like trying to grab a ham. He was huge!

Car #4: One of my friends had an Austin Healy Sprite – right hand drive. A European version, the driver sat on the right side. After the gig in Baltimore, he had the Austin's top down and put one of the large band speakers on the left seat of the car. All the way home, from behind, it looked like that box was driving. Five days later, I owned that car. He sold it to me for $950. A 1964 Red Austin Healy Sprite Roadster.

1964 Austin Healy Sprite

Before I knew it, it was time to return to Pensacola. My cousin, John, drove with me to Florida. I dropped him off in Jacksonville and then drove across the panhandle to Pensacola. The road from Maryland to Florida had many speed limit changes. During the trip to Jacksonville, we made the mistake of not slowing down coming into one of the many little towns in Georgia. No super highways in those days. A Georgia State Policeman stopped us (me) for speeding and said I would have to come back to this town in a month to stand trial unless I paid him the $20 fine. I paid it, not sure if this policeman was on the take or not, but I did not want to have tell Sergeant Washington that I got a ticket and had to go back to Georgia. I could just imagine the "fire and brimstone" from that exchange.

Graduation

Friday, January 12, 1968 was commissioning day. All of the candidate officers lined up with their battalions for a commissioning parade, honoring all the soon-to-be ensigns. There was a band playing marching songs as we paraded across the field, adding

Graduation Parade for Class 38-67

to the pomp of the day. After a few speeches about Navy tradition and our training, "Pass in Review" was ordered and one by one we led our battalions past the reviewing stand. "Eyes right" as we approached the admiral on the stand, rendering him appropriate honors, as he saluted us back. Then it was over, except for the official commissioning.

The commissioning was done in a building adjacent to the parade ground. We were all given the "Oath of Office" and declared "Officers and Gentlemen" by Act of Congress.

Prior to the commissioning, my mother, who had flown down from Baltimore the day before, pointed out that I had cut my right ear with the sword I was carrying. I hadn't really learned to use it in parade very well. I was my own first casualty.

Ensign is the lowest commissioned officer rank in the Navy, equivalent to 2nd Lieutenant in the Army. Ensigns wear a single gold bar on their collars and because of this, they are often

Ensign Marty Herzog with Mom

referred to as "Butter-bars." After the commissioning ceremony, all the new ensigns from class 38-67 lined up at the door to exit the building and receive a ceremonial, traditional first salute. Tradition states that the first person to salute a newly commissioned officer is to receive a silver dollar from that officer. I had my silver dollar in my pocket. As we left the building, who was standing outside the door? ... Gunnery Sergeant Washington, smiling, as proud as can be. Standing at attention, with his right-hand saluting each of us as we left and his left hand out to receive the silver dollar from each of us. Then he shook our hand and wished us good luck with flight school. It was a proud moment for all of us.

With mixed emotions, I left the area, feeling a bit strange to not be going back to the barracks, but to the Bachelor Officer Quarters or B.O.Q. After I took my mom back to the airport, I drove my Austin Healy back by the Battalion Three barracks. Many memories over the last three and a half months. Wait! – Is that Sergeant Grelish and

Sergeant Washington walking toward me? Were they going to salute me? Smiling, they did and I, also smiling, smartly returned their salute from inside my car and continued on my way. But something seemed strange. Were my eyes playing tricks on me? Salutes are given with right hands. Did they just give me left-handed salutes? Wouldn't that be just like them?

CHAPTER 3

FLIGHT TRAINING

January 1968 – May 1969

Events in the Navy and worldwide during this time

October 11, 1968   Apollo 7
The first manned Apollo mission was launched. Wally Schirra,
Donn Eisele, Walter Cunningham

January 14, 1969   USS Enterprise fire
The fire broke out after a Zuni rocket exploded. Subsequent
fire and explosions blew holes in the flight deck. 28 were
killed, 314 injured, 15 aircraft were destroyed.

Ground School - Pensacola

No more marching, no rifle, no poopy suits…all things of the
recent past. Next, I had to deal with Pre-Flight Ground School and, as
is clear by now, school had never been a strong point for me. At least,
the subjects in this school had to do with relevant elements of my life:
Aviation Physiology, Meteorology, Aerodynamics, Weapons Systems,
Aircraft Recognition, and Leadership. After several more weeks of
sitting in a classroom, we would finally begin flight training.

But before flight training, we also had to endure some more water survival training:

1) One-mile swim: Sixty of us in the pool at the same time. We had to swim from one end of the pool to the other, for what seemed like an infinite number of laps, while wearing a flight suit. Fortunately, we didn't have to wear our flight boots. A mile is a long way to swim, especially with all of those bodies in the way. We ended up unintentionally kicking each other, splashing each other, and bumping into each other. It was a real ordeal, but we only had to do it once. So, we just had to bear it and get it over with.

2) Drown-proofing: We had to stay afloat without touching anything or anyone for 15 minutes. That wasn't so bad, but we weren't allowed to paddle or kick our feet either. Drown-proofing was a technique used to stay alive if you were injured, using the air in your lungs for buoyancy. You would take a deep breath and allow your head and body to rest on the water (head face down). Then when you needed to, you would lift your head up to exhale and take a deep breath. When you exhaled and inhaled, you would settle under the water. Then the air inside of you would eventually bring you back to the surface (head face down again), where you would hang out until you needed to take another breath and repeat the process. It was quite hard to master this, but after a while most of us got the hang of it.

3) Tower Jump: We had to simulate jumping off a ship ... abandoning ship. It was only a 20-foot tower but it seemed much higher when you actually got up there. You were to cross your arms (holding your nose was optional) step off the platform, and as you were falling you were supposed to cross your legs, ankle over ankle. Crossing your legs was supposed to protect your groin area should you land on something in or under the water.

4) Dilbert Dunker: This trainer simulated a crash landing in the water. You would get seated in the "Dunker," which was a simulated aircraft cockpit with a seat, shoulder straps, and a seat belt. When you were ready, the Dunker would be released to

slide about 15 feet down a 45-degree rail into the water. When it hit the water it would stop, and then rotate forward, flipping the pilot over and then it would settle toward the bottom of the pool with the pilot upside down. When the bubbles subsided, the pilot was supposed to get oriented, unfasten his straps, pull himself out of the cockpit (which took him deeper into the water) and then swim to the surface. It wasn't too hard to do, once you got over the anxiety of being jerked around by the apparatus.

5) Parachute drag: This test was to simulate releasing yourself from a parachute while being pulled through the water by wind. We wore a torso harness, a flight item worn by pilots which was attached to the straps of the parachute in your airplane. The parachute straps were attached to our torso harnesses using Koch (pronounced "coke") fittings. These fittings could be easily disconnected, once you knew how. You would simply push the cover up and pull the release fitting down and the strap would be freed. For the training, we were to stand on the edge of the pool facing away from the water with our arms crossed over our chests. The parachute straps were connected to a winch, which pulled us over backwards into the pool. Once we were moving, we were to release the fittings and free ourselves from the straps. Piece of cake!

Pensacola Beach

One nice thing about ground school was that at 1600 (4:00 PM) we were generally finished for the day and could go "home." For my two roommates and me, home was at 1408 Ariola Drive, on Pensacola Beach. We lived right on the Gulf. Only a sliding glass door separated

1408 Ariola Drive

us from the sand and the Gulf of Mexico. What could be better? The beautiful blue gulf water and squeaky-clean sand were right outside our door.

Our neighbor was a flight surgeon who was going through his training as well. His training was quite similar to ours, but not quite as intense. "Doc" was a cardiologist, but he was also a drummer. Since I was a guitarist, we got along quite well.

We did a lot of jammin'.

Looking out the back door

Primary Prop Training - Pensacola

After completing ground school and swim survival, we reported to VT-1 (Training Squadron One), the next step in our journey towards being designated Naval Aviators. Before our first flight, we spent more hours in the classroom, learning flight procedures and course rules for flying out of Saufley Field, our new home. We had to spend some hours familiarizing ourselves with the cockpit layout of the T-34B "Mentor", the propeller aircraft that we would be flying soon.

Our first test was the blindfold cockpit check. We would sit in a dummy cockpit trainer which was just like sitting in the cockpit of the real airplane. It had all of the switches and gauges and knobs, etc. that were in the actual aircraft. Our instructor, standing outside the trainer, would have us close our eyes and point to or touch various cockpit gauges and switches: Altimeter, Airspeed Indicator, V.S.I. (Vertical Speed Indicator), Magneto Switch, and so forth.

My instructor was Lieutenant Hodgon. He was very nice and seemed to understand the anxiety I had, since I had never piloted an aircraft before. We flew 11 "hops" together. A "hop" was a shorthand way of referring to an instructional flight.

On my third hop, as I was climbing out after take-off, the aircraft would not attain the standard 110-knot climb. If I held 110 knots at full power, the aircraft would actually descend. It just wouldn't climb. If I raised the nose to climb, the speed would fall below 110 knots. I was quite perplexed. What's wrong? I went through several cycles of raising and lowering the nose of my trusty T-34 before LT Hogdon (from the back seat) asked me if I thought that maybe I had forgotten something. This was only my third hop and I was so disoriented and confused that I'm not sure that I could have remembered my middle name at that point.

Lt Hogdon said, "OK, Marty, put your hand on the landing gear handle," which I did. Oh, that's what's wrong! The landing gear handle was still down! I had never raised my landing gear. How embarrassing! I quickly remedied that and attained my 110-knot climb. It was much easier once the landing gear was up.

A student's twelfth hop was a check flight to determine if he was "safe for solo." The twelve-check, as it was called, was given by a different instructor, not your primary instructor. He ran you through all of the items that you should have learned to do, but most importantly, he needed to be convinced that you could land and take off safely. The instructor checked your inflight procedures and observed several of your landings, and if he thought you were safe, he would actually get out of the aircraft at an outlying field and watch you do three or four more landings solo, before he got back in for the trip home. That was your clue that you had passed. If he got out, then you were "safe for solo." If he didn't, … well, that wasn't so good. After arriving back at Saufley, if you were safe for solo, you would be scheduled for your solo flight.

"Soloing" was a cause for celebration. Every Friday, all the students who had soloed that week, "reported" to the Officers Club for ceremonial tie cutting. The students would have their ties cut about 3-4 inches from

Solo Pilot -- Ensign Marty Herzog

the knot by their instructor. My solo was March 27, 1968. It was my thirteenth flight, ever. Lucky Thirteen.

After soloing, there were six flights remaining at VT-1. These were acrobatic hops. We would take the T-34 through Loops, Spins, Half Cuban Eights, Immelmanns, Aileron Rolls and Barrel Rolls. I loved it. Now this was really fun!

After nineteen flights in Primary Flight Training, we were finished. The next step would be Basic Flight Training in either jets, helos, or props. Several weeks prior to our last hop in Primary, each of us selected the kind of aircraft we would like to fly and then based on our grades, we would be assigned to one of the three communities. I wanted jets. The grade cut-off for jets was 3.06. I had a 3.07. I made it! For my next assignment, I would be sent to Meridian, Mississippi to learn to fly the T-2A Buckeye jet aircraft.

Basic Jet Training – Meridian, Mississippi

I packed up and said goodbye to my beach home in Pensacola and headed for Meridian, Mississippi in my Austin Healy. Finding no place to live in Meridian that was as cool as Pensacola Beach, I stayed at the B.O.Q. (Bachelor Officer Quarters) for the next four and a half months.

Car #5 - By then, I had gotten tired of driving the Austin Healy. Even though it was a really neat car to drive, the little Sprite had its drawbacks. For example, when seated behind the wheel, you were sitting less than 12 inches from the street. Also, being so low, it was hard to see past other cars on the road. So, I traded my Healy in for a maroon 1965 "396" Chevy Camaro. This car had power…more than any car I had ever driven. I wasn't used to "leaving a patch" of rubber when accelerating. This car had "four on the floor." – four gears with a standard shift on the console between the driver's seat and the passenger's seat. This car could leave a patch of rubber on the road in all four gears, without even trying. It just wanted to go fast all by itself. I knew that it wouldn't be long before I would have a collection of tickets from the local police.

Now it was time for jets, but the first stop was more ground school, several weeks of learning about the systems in the T-2A "Buckeye."

Along with the classroom training, we were given several other special training experiences:

1) Ejection Trainer – In a special area of the VT-7 hanger, one by one, we strapped into a seat, similar to the Buckeye ejection seat. The seat was mounted on rails. Then, we were shown where the ejection handles were: one between your legs for ejection when you had very little time to get ready and one over your head called the "face curtain" for when you had more time to safely position yourself for the ejection that would ensue.

   After a dry run or two, the techs told us they were arming the seat. They would back off a safe distance and yell "EJECT!", whereupon you were to smartly pull the face curtain down with both hands over your helmet to your lap. This activated a charge that ejected you and the seat about 30 feet up the rails that the seat was attached to. This trip took a fraction of a second, just to give us some small sense of what it was like to eject.

   We were a little uneasy when they told us that we had only experienced a "half charge." A real ejection would be much more violent.

2) Low Pressure Trainer – This trainer was to familiarize us with oxygen masks and the effects of being without oxygen at high altitude. About 20 of us sat in a cylinder- shaped trainer along with 6 instructors. The hatch was closed and the room was sealed. After adjusting our oxygen masks and breathing through them for a little while, it was announced: "Low pressure training commencing."

   There was a surgeon's plastic glove tied in a knot at the wrist, hanging from the ceiling. The pressure in the room was lowered by pumping air out of the room. This simulated being at higher altitudes, where there was less oxygen. Soon, the glove inflated to the size of a balloon.

   When we reached a pressure that simulated being at 40,000 feet, we paired up and one member of each pair would remove his oxygen mask and do a simple task. This task was to take a deck of cards and separate it into four piles containing all the same suit, hearts, diamonds, clubs and spades while not wearing your oxygen mask. This was easy at first. However, after about two minutes, our coordination started to fail and we couldn't put the cards where we wanted them and what's more, we couldn't figure out how to sort them, a real demonstration of the effect of being without oxygen. Our partner's job was to help us refasten our oxygen masks when we had lost the ability to sort the cards, since our hand coordination would quite possibly be lost at that point. As soon as our oxygen was restored, we recovered. We learned that without oxygen at high altitude, our brains would only function for a short time. After that, we would be incapacitated.

3) Night Vision Trainer: In this trainer, we were seated in a brightly lit room. The lights were turned off and we were asked to look at the wall in front of us. None of us could see anything on the wall. After 10 minutes of sitting in the dark, our eyes "dark adapted" and we could see the faint images that were on the wall in front of us. Some red lights were turned on, and we noted that we were still able to see the images on the wall. Then white lights were turned on and off and we immediately lost our night vision. We could no longer see the images on the wall. Then the white lights of the room were gradually turned back on and we were finished with the exercise. We learned the importance of using only red light if we wanted to see in the dark and the importance of giving our eyes time to "dark adapt" before flying at night.

Before our first flight, we were issued some special equipment and taught how to use it:

1) Torso harness: We had used these in Pensacola for the parachute drag trainer. To put this on, you would have to put your legs through the "foot holes" like a pair of trousers without pant legs, pulling it up and then putting your arms through similar "shoulder holes" and then cinching it all down. It was supposed to fit snuggly.

In the aircraft, the torso harness would attach to the ejection seat and parachute at four places, two at the shoulder and two at over our thighs near the waist. The purpose of the torso harness was to hold the pilot close to the ejection seat during an ejection sequence and of course, to remain connected to the parachute when it automatically deployed.

Marty modeling jet flight gear

2) G-suit. Actually, this would be the first piece of flight gear to be put on. It was made of rubber and fabric, personally sized to fit each individual aviator. It had three vertical zippers. To put it on, you would wrap it around your waist and zip the first zipper, on the side. It should be snug. Then the next two zippers closed the leg pieces and ran from your ankle up the inside of your leg to your crotch. The g- suit was connected in the airplane to an air system that inflated bladders in the g-suit when you were "pulling g's". An inflated g-suit would help keep a pilot's blood from pooling in his lower extremities, allowing the pilot to withstand higher g forces. If a pilot's blood was allowed to pool in the lower extremities, it would obviously not be in critical parts of the upper body, such as the brain and eyes. Insufficient blood flow in a pilot's eyes would cause him to black-out (lose his vision) and insufficient blood flow in the brain would cause him to eventually lose consciousness.

3) Survival vest: The vest hung over your shoulders and contained various items that you should have with you in a survival situation, should you have to eject in a remote or hostile area. In Vietnam, we generally carried a pistol in our vest in addition to standard survival items such as a knife, flares, water bottles, first aid supplies and so forth.

4) Oxygen mask: A standard mask would attach to our helmets. As students, these were worn from the time we started the aircraft until we shut it down.

My first jet flight was on May 3, 1968 with marine Captain Shultz. He was very understanding and a compassionate, patient teacher…a great instructor. Once again, there were 11 familiarization flights followed by a 12 check and a solo.

The T-2A was a single engine jet. Since the T-2 was a bit underpowered, it was always a briefing item to discuss how much runway should be needed for takeoff on that day's flight. As we were taking off, we were supposed

T2-A Buckeye

to monitor our airspeed and the amount of runway remaining as we were rolling. Warmer weather made takeoff distances greater and each day in Meridian seemed to be getting warmer as summer approached. N.A.S. Meridian's McCain Field had 8000 feet of runway and that was usually enough for a normal takeoff.

In VT-7 (Training Squadron Seven), we also learned jet acrobatics, followed by "bag" hops. These were instrument training flights. The bag was a white opaque piece of plastic material that attached to the inside of the aft canopy. It would snap on the canopy at six points, so that when the canopy was closed, the back-seat pilot would not be able to see out. The instructor pilot would sit in the front seat in the clear, while the student pilot in the back seat would be "under the bag." He would be in simulated instrument conditions…no horizon and no visible cues as to the attitude of his aircraft. Once the canopy was closed, he would have to use and depend on the instruments in front of him on the cockpit instrument panel. There were two kinds of "bag" hops: Basic Instruments or B.I. hops and Radio Instruments or R.I. hops, which involved navigation.

After instrument training, we were transferred to VT-9 (Training Squadron Nine) for night familiarization and two plane and four plane formation. VT-7 and VT-9 were housed in the same hangar, so the transfer involved only a walk down the hall. After my last formation flight on August 30, it was time to return to Pensacola for air-to-air gunnery and carrier qualifications (C.Q.)

Back to the Beach

When I got back to Pensacola, I remembered that the best place to live in Pensacola was at the beach. Another flight student, Pete Frederick and I rented a house at 1006 Ariola Drive for our brief stay at VT-4 (Training Squadron Four). This house was built on stilts and concrete blocks. We lived on the second level and parked underneath. It was great to be back in Pensacola.

1006 Ariola Drive

Car #6 - My Camaro had gotten me into trouble a few times, so I decided it was time to down-size. I bought a 1968 yellow Fiat 124 Spider, my first-ever brand-new car. It cost $3500, which doesn't sound like much in today's economy, but it was a lot in 1968.

1968 Fiat Spider

Guns

On the VT-4 flight line we saw more T-2s. They looked like the same jets we flew in Meridian, but they were actually quite different.

These planes, T-2Bs, had two engines and a lot more get-up-and-go. My first flight in the "B" was September 26, 1968. And, after four familiarization or "Fam" flights, we were ready for air-to-air gunnery.

Gunnery stage consisted of ten flights. Five were dual. Five were solo. My instructor was Air Force Lieutenant Colonel Butler. I had been very fortunate, since nearly every instructor I had flown with had been super. Colonel Butler was no exception.

The air to air gunnery pattern had the shape of a slanted figure eight with the top of the eight at 15,000 feet and the bottom at 12,000 feet. An aircraft called the "tractor" would tow the target banner at 150 knots, 12,000 feet, and its pilot would act as the range safety officer. The banner, made of a meshy canvas material - 40 feet long - 7 ½ feet high, was towed on cables behind the tractor. It was white with a four-foot diameter red bull's eye right in the middle.

It's pretty hard to describe the gun pattern, so I won't attempt to do it here. Let it suffice to say that it was the most challenging flying we had done to date, but it was really rewarding and exciting. We actually fired live ammunition. After firing the guns, you could smell cordite in the cockpit. It did something to your insides. Adrenaline? We were really doing something tactical now.

U.S.S. Lexington – CVT-16

C.Q. (Carrier Qualification) – Our next phase of training prepared us for our first arrested landings on an aircraft carrier. We were scheduled for two dual flights and then eight solo flights at a nearby practice landing field. These flights were strictly landing practice. There were 6-8 pilots in the oval shaped landing pattern, practicing for the eventual trip to the aircraft carrier.

We already knew how to land an airplane but landing on an aircraft carrier required much more precision. There was a very small area in which we had to place the wheels of our jet and we needed to be at the proper speed and glide slope angle and lined up correctly. Small deviations were acceptable. The key word here is "small." Too much deviation could lead to damage to the aircraft or even worse, an accident.

We worked with our L.S.O. (Landing Signal Officer), a specially trained instructor who would grade us and help us, talking to us by radio as we were landing. He stood next to the runway, adjacent to where our jets should touch down, helping us by giving instructions such as "a little power" (add a judicious amount of power – not a lot) or "You're going high" (advisory – warning you that you should watch your altitude on the glide slope. If you didn't make an adjustment, you would be high soon), "Meatball, line-up, and angle of attack" were the three main items of our scan as we were landing.

> The "Meatball" was a yellow ball of light projected from a lens on the ground adjacent to our landing area. The "ball" would appear to move up and down between two horizontal rows of green lights, called datum lights. If the ball appeared above the datums you were high, below meant you were low. Optimally, you wanted the ball to be perfectly between the datums – right in the middle.

> "Line–up" on a carrier was critical and difficult to keep up with since the carrier was moving while you were landing. You were landing on what was called an "angled deck." The landing area angles about 10 degrees from the main axis of the ship. So, when you were on final approach and on centerline of the landing area, your landing spot was moving to your right. You were essentially landing on a moving target. This could not be simulated at a field and was experienced for the first time at the carrier.

> "Angle of Attack" is the angle the wings of your aircraft make with the air flow over them while flying. It correlates to airspeed. It is important that the aircraft

has the right attitude (or angle of attack) when touching down. If your nose is too low, the nose wheel could land first – not good. If the nose was too high, the tail hook could catch the cross-deck pendant (the arresting wire) before the main wheels touch down - also not good. If this happened, the aircraft could be jerked out of the sky and slammed to the deck – most likely damaging the jet and perhaps injuring the pilot.

The pilot's scan: "Meatball, Line-up, Angle of attack"

Each time around the landing pattern, the L.S.O. would grade our landings. After these 10 training flights, the L.S.O. would hopefully declare you ready. Then it was off to "Lady Lex." *Lexington* was an old World War Two carrier with a wooden flight deck that had been converted into a carrier that was used exclusively for carrier landing practice.

On November 13, 1968, I was in a group of four students, that took off from Pensacola and proceeded with a safety pilot (a seasoned instructor) to the Lex for carrier qualification. Each of the four students was a solo. No one in his right mind would go with a student pilot for his first arrested landing. (Arrested landings were called "traps" by naval aviators.)

November 13th was my 23rd birthday! As we were flying out to the ship, I was a bit anxious. You might say, I was scared. I had a vision of my tombstone:

Martin Herzog
Born: November 13, 1945
Died: November 13, 1968

Was this some kind of omen?

The first two passes at the ship were to be touch and goes, Tailhook up. When you touched down on the flight deck, you would advance the throttles to full power to take off and go around again. After my 2 touch and goes, the L.S.O. said to me "405, drop your hook." "405, Wilco," was my reply, acknowledging that I would lower my tailhook. The next three landings were traps (arrested landings), followed by a short taxi forward on the flight deck and a catapult shot.

After landing, the yellow shirted flight deck personnel signaled me where to taxi on the flight deck. They were very skilled at giving directions. A good thing – because this was my first time, taxiing a jet on the flight deck of a carrier and the flight deck seemed very small. The taxi directors guided me up to the catapult for launch.

After a few external checks by the ground crew, I completed the take-off check list and got positioned on the catapult mechanism. Then it was "whoosh" – down the catapult track and into the air again. Wow! What a feeling! Acceleration! A catapult shot is better than any Disneyland ride you can imagine. Zero to 120 knots in one and a half seconds. Yaahoooo!

Before we knew it, we were "carrier qualed" and on the way back to Pensacola, having accomplished something that only Navy and Marine pilots do! Now we could truly call ourselves "Naval Aviators."

Advanced Jet Training – Beeville, Texas

After my T-2B carrier qualification flight, I packed up my Fiat and left beautiful Pensacola Beach and was off to Naval Air Station Chase Field, Beeville, Texas for Advanced Jet Training. The past 10 months were a blur in my memory. My goal of being designated a Naval Aviator would be realized in Beeville.

When I reported aboard VT-25 (Training Squadron Two Five), I was ready and eager to fly a different jet – the F-9 "Cougar," but I found that more ground school was required first: Aerodynamics, Flight Rules, Instrument Rules, Meteorology, Navigation, Radar, Safety and Survival. Then it was time to fly. Advanced Jet Training was comprised of over 100 flights in 12 stages lettered A through L.

A Student Naval Aviator, or simply S.N.A., would have the same instructor for nearly every flight in the first four stages. My primary instructor was Lieutenant, Junior Grade Peter Batcheller. Pete was a SERGRAD, (SElectively Retained GRADuate of the Naval Flight Program.) Six months ago, Pete was in the same place I was in now. He was in A.O.C.S. (Aviation Officer Candidate School) class 15-67. I was in 38-67 (23 weeks behind him). Pete was a real top-notch guy, very friendly and understanding – a great instructor.

A Stage - Familiarization

Pete Batcheller (Picture by permission of Peter Batcheller)

Pete led me through the five Fam hops in A Stage. My first flight in the F-9 was on January 9, 1969. After my six- check flight with a different instructor, I soloed the "T," – the TF-9J, the two-seat F-9. There was a single seat version of the F-9 as well.

The F-9 was a real fun airplane to fly, once you actually got it airborne. But that was the challenge, getting it airborne. Below 300 knots, the F-9 was "a dog." It took a lot of runway just to get it airborne. However, at 300 knots and above, the F-9 was a "hot airplane." It was very responsive and was a good fighter. In J stage (Air-to-Air Tactics), we found that keeping the F-9 above 300 knots was a key to success.

The F-9 was an old aircraft. It was used in the Korean War and was nearing the end of its time. You might simply say; the jets were getting "tired." We always looked them over carefully on pre-flight, before getting in to fly. They almost always would have puddles of hydraulic fluid under

TF-9J Cougar

them where seals had loosened over the years and the hydraulic fluid dripped out after the engine was shut down. This wasn't a big problem, because once the engine was started again, the hydraulic pressure would rise which would tighten the seals and then everything would work fine. As long as nothing was leaking after starting the jet, it was a "GO" for flight. There was a joke going around that if you didn't see hydraulic fluid under your jet when you walked up to it, it was probably empty and needed to have hydraulic fluid put in it before flying.

After A Stage, I went on to B and C Stage, again with Pete as my instructor. By now, I was a Lieutenant, Junior Grade myself, the same rank as Pete. I had been promoted on January 12, 1968 (one year to the day after commissioning in Pensacola). So much had happened since then.

B Stage - Basic Instruments
C Stage - Radio Instruments

B and C Stage were instrument training hops – "under the bag" again. After my C-18X (eighteen check), I was awarded my Standard Instrument Card. This card gave me permission to fly in I.F.R. conditions without an instructor (I.F.R. = Instrument Flight Rules - in the clouds – low visibility). Once a student received that card, there was so much more that he could do. Most of our flying required good visibility. Now that I was no longer bound to the "Blue Sky" flights, I could fly solo through the clouds to weather that was "clear on top" or above the clouds.

D Stage – Re-Familiarization

D Stage involved another safe-for-solo check flight so I could fly the "A." The AF-9J was the single seat version of the F-9. It was really cool. This was the first time I flew an aircraft that was actually made for one pilot. My first flight in the "A" was February 24, 1969.

E Stage - Formation
F Stage - Night Familiarization

The next two stages E and F Stage were formation and night familiarization flights. It was in mid-March when a reality of aviation hit me between the eyes. Flying, especially tactical flying was inherently dangerous.

One night in March, another student, a good friend of mine named Ed Herdrich, crashed in the landing pattern at Chase Field about 2 miles from the runway. Ed was in A.O.C.S. class 40-67 (2 weeks after me.) It was a pitch-black night and we speculated that he got disoriented and lost his bearings. He crashed in a wings level attitude and was killed. I was honored to be his escort when his remains were sent to Phoenix for interment on March 24, 1969.

G Stage - Low Level Navigation
H Stage - Solo Cross-country (Out and In)

Flying can be unforgiving. Why some pilots like Ed are killed and others are not remains a mystery to me. Looking back on my career, I can recall several times that I could have had the same fate as Ed but was spared.

One of our classmates was a marine First Lieutenant who had been dubbed "Mad Dog." Mad Dog was a wild man. He would often get intoxicated at the O-Club (Officer's Club) and do wild, outlandish things while under the influence. Most of us thought he was just a little bit "over the edge," but he was funny and reckless, a dangerous combination for a pilot. He had somehow managed to survive the dangers of flying up to this point, but how he had done that was a mystery. He was just too wild.

H stage involved an "out and in" flight, a solo flight to a base hundreds of miles away, perhaps in Oklahoma or Louisiana. The jet would be refueled and the pilot would then fly it back to Beeville. The idea was for the pilot to experience an instrument flight to an unfamiliar base and back, all by himself. These flights were often done on Saturdays or Sundays when the instructors were relaxing at home with their families.

This particular Sunday, Mad Dog was scheduled for his "out and in." He told us that when he got back to the field, he was going to do something spectacular. He even told us about what time to expect him. I wasn't going to miss this. At the designated time, I drove into the base from the trailer where I was living and sat down at the Officers Club pool to wait and watch. There were quite a few other students there as well, waiting for this "spectacular event."

Normally when we returned to the field for landing, we flew next to a little town called Normanna at 1200 feet and 300 knots. This was almost a perfect direct line to runway 13 at Chase Field about 12 miles out. From Normanna, the course rules stated that we were to fly in at 300 knots and "break" at midfield (halfway down the runway). A break meant you would roll the jet about 45-60 degrees, retard the throttle, extend the speed brakes and pull the jet around through 180 degrees maintaining 1200 feet altitude, all the while slowing down to the allowable speed to extend landing gear and flaps for landing.

After 180 degrees of turn, the aircraft should be almost slow enough to land. The pilot would go through landing checklists and request permission to land from the tower. After clearance from the Tower, the pilot would commence a descending 180 degree turn to line up with the runway and eventually land, roll out to the end of the runway, and then taxi to the flight line. That was normal. But today, things would not be normal. It was Mad Dog out there.

So, from our vantage point at the pool, we waited. Then we heard a jet. It had to be Mad Dog. The jet sounded a little bit strange. Higher pitched than usual. "He must be going fast," someone said. We all had good eyesight and were scanning the horizon trying to spot him. "He should be coming from Normanna," another pilot shouted. The sound was getting louder, not really loud, but louder. The pitch of the sound was rising. He was getting closer. But no one could see him. "We should see him by now." "Where is he?"

"There he is!" one of the observers shouted. We looked at the observer and he was pointing nearly straight up in the air. We looked up and there was an orange and white F-9, (all of our F-9s were orange and white) with shock waves coming off its wings. He was nearly supersonic. It was coming almost straight down, not actually at 90 degrees but about 70 degrees, heading toward the runway. Then he started pulling up. He's going to make it. Sure enough, by the time he was over the runway, he was level, but he was flying that jet into the break faster than I ever saw an F-9 go before.

When he reached midfield, he rolled into a steeper turn than the normal 60 degrees of bank and throttled back but after 180 degrees of turn that jet was still going too fast to put the landing gear down – way too fast. Then he did something I have never seen before or since. He continued around to make a complete circle, still going pretty fast but significantly slower now. On his second time around, he was slow enough to lower the landing gear and land the jet.

We all jumped in our cars and headed for the flight line. When we got there, there was Mad Dog triumphantly taxiing into the line area with both hands out of the cockpit giving us two thumbs up. The plane captain, an enlisted man who helped with parking the jet, gave him the stop signal and then put chocks in front of and behind his wheels. The plane captain then gave Mad Dog the signal to shut down the engine. When Mad Dog brought the throttle back "around the horn" to shut down the engine, you could see the jet visibly sag. Someone said, "He killed it." Then as the engine continued to wind down, the plane started spurting hydraulic fluid in all directions. "He really killed it," the same guy noted. I had never seen a plane die before and could not imagine what that might have looked like, but now I knew. This one died right in front of us, courtesy of Mad Dog.

In today's Navy, an incident like this would most likely lead to the pilot's dismissal from the flight training program. However, in those days, the Navy needed all the pilots they could get, so Mad Dog continued with his flight training and eventually was awarded his wings. Nothing was said about this incident. It may be interesting to note that I met Mad Dog about four years later at the Officer's Club in Miramar, California. He had recently finished an assignment with the Marines in Vietnam, flying F-4 Phantoms. I was really surprised to see him again.

Sadly, a few years later, I heard that he had been killed in an auto accident.

I Stage – Air to Ground Weapons
J Stage – Air to Air Tactics

The next stages were really exciting and tactical.

> I Stage was air to ground weapons. We dropped 25-pound practice bombs (Mark 76's) on a target range using 30-degree and 45-degree bombing runs. We also shot 2.75" rockets.

> J Stage was Air to Air tactics – Top Gun stuff – one pilot versus another or two-on-one. A.C.M. Air Combat Maneuvering.

The check flight in J Stage was a one-on-one "fight" with an instructor. Student versus Instructor. I really wanted to win that fight, but the instructors had so much experience, I knew that it wasn't likely.

The fight would begin with the two opposing aircraft flying towards each other at 400+ knots. Neither pilot had positional advantage. The instructor would announce "The fight's on," and it began. Normally, at that point, the jets would pass each other heading in opposite directions and then turn into each other trying to turn harder than the opposition so to gain advantage by getting behind him "at his six o'clock." This kind of turning continued until one pilot realized that he was losing advantage, then he would try another maneuver to regain the advantage. This maneuvering continued until one pilot was clearly the winner.

I knew if I did the normal stuff, I would most likely lose. Most of the instructors had been doing this for years. I had decided what I was going to do before we even took off. I realized that for a moment when the jets passed each other at high speed, we each lost visual contact with each other. My plan was to do something the instructor didn't expect at that instant.

When it was time for our one-on-one fight, the instructor and I were side by side in formation (same direction). He said "Smacker two, take separation." I returned with "Two, Wilco." Taking separation meant that we would each advance our throttle to full power and turn 45 degrees away from the present flight path, one jet turning right, the other turning left. We flew for a while at this 90-degree angle and then "Smacker Two, turn in", "Wilco."

That meant we were to smoothly turn our aircraft to head directly at each other while assuring that the throttle was at full power. ("OK, Marty," I said to myself…. "not too hard. Don't want to bleed off your airspeed.") When we were nose to nose and about 1000 feet apart, the instructor said "Smackers, fight's on." We passed left to left. I looked down at my airspeed indicator and I had nearly 450 knots on my jet and full power. Perfect! Power would stay at full for the entire evolution. Energy was important in A.C.M. (Air Combat Maneuvering).

When we passed each other, I initially turned left, in case he was looking in his mirrors. When I went into his "blind area," I rolled out and pulled back on the stick to go vertical. I was planning on doing a loop, re-acquiring Smacker One somewhere over the top, hopefully with him in his level circle looking for me on his altitude.

Then I saw him. He was right where I thought he would be. I floated a little inverted at the top of my loop and was calculating when I would continue to pull to get to his six. Then, "Smacker Two, do you have a tally?" (He wanted to know if I had visual contact with his aircraft. Haaa! He didn't see me or he wouldn't have asked.) I was sweating profusely by now but couldn't help smiling inside my oxygen mask. I wanted to wipe my face but I wasn't coming off the controls. No way! I answered him, "Affirmative." He said, "Well I guess you've got the advantage." Now I knew I had him. I could imagine him looking all around for me. He was still in a steep left turn, varying his angle of bank, looking for me at the altitude he was flying, not up where I was, several thousand feet higher. By now I had positioned myself above and behind him and was beginning to track. When he saw me, he started to turn harder, but it was too late. One "high yo-yo" (a tactical maneuver) and I had him! I broadcast, "Fox Two," which meant I would have fired a missile. He said "Fight's over, good job, Smacker Two." I had won. Maybe one day, I'll be a fighter pilot.

K Stage – Air to Air Gunnery

Gunnery in the F-9 was pretty much the same as gunnery in the T-2 except the pattern was bigger, the G's were higher and the speeds were faster.

Just a year or so prior, training command gunnery had been done in the F-11 "Tiger," the same jet that the Blue Angels were flying in 1968-69. The F-11 was a super-hot airplane, probably more than a student could handle. It had one single engine with afterburner. Also, it was supersonic. Quite a lot of airplane for a student. It made me wish that I had gone through my training a year ago. I would have had the opportunity to fly it. There was a story going around about an F-11 student flying one of his solo hops in the gunnery pattern.

He was complaining to the instructor, who was towing the banner, that he was having a hard time controlling his jet in the gunnery pattern. The instructor told him to depart the pattern and head for the beach to land. (Air to air gunnery was flown in a safe area over the Gulf of Mexico.) He also said, "Be sure to slow flight the airplane and when you get back to the field, do a straight in approach." The instructor was telling him to be sure that he could handle the airplane at slow speeds, just in case it was structurally damaged. A straight in would be an approach with minimal turns – giving you the best opportunity for a safe landing.

When he got back to Chase Field, he told the tower he was declaring an emergency. When he had slowed the airplane to try to extend the landing gear, it became very hard to control. He couldn't get slow enough to extend the landing gear and he was having a hard time keeping the wings level even at higher speeds. In addition, he had a hydraulic failure and was flying "manual." Tower told him to maintain safe flying speed and fly over the runway at 1200 feet. They would "put the binoculars on him to see if they could spot any damage." They were amazed at what they saw. Tower said, "5-1-1 can you see your wings?" (pause) "Uhhh no. I can't."

They asked because they couldn't see them either. The pilot of 511 was directed to a safe area and told to eject. When the aircraft was recovered, they noted that there were no ailerons on it. The pilot was "steering" with his rudder only. The wings had broken off in the gunnery pattern at the wing fold position. He had less than half a wing on each side.

It was quite a feat that he was able to fly that jet at all and even more incredible that he made it back to the field. I never met him and don't remember his name. He was gone by the time I showed up at VT-25, but the story was amazing. It's always interesting to hear how pilots get their call signs and nicknames. I was told that his call sign from then on was "Bullet."

L Stage – Carrier Qualification

Advanced Jet Training Carrier Quals was my hardest phase. I got two downs in L Stage. A "down" is an unsatisfactory flight where the student shows unsafe tendencies or below average progress. My downs came at the field – not at the carrier.

Most of our training in L stage took place at an outlying field called N.A.L.F. Goliad (Naval Auxiliary Landing Field Goliad). Goliad was about 15 miles northeast of Beeville and was used primarily for landing practice, so it was ideal for our preparation for carrier qualification. During the intense work- up period, eight aircraft would be flown to Goliad on a morning flight from Beeville. They would be used at Goliad all day and then flown back in the late afternoon. The student pilots would be shuttled back and forth between Beeville and Goliad by bus.

Operations were fast paced at Goliad and sometimes things were carelessly overlooked on preflight or startup checks. On one flight after I taxied out for take-off, was cleared and took off, the L.S.O. called me on the radio and said, "5-0-1, carefully reach over your head and remove the safety pins to your ejection seat." That was it – my first down. With the safety pins in, I wouldn't be able to eject if the need arose. The safety pins are always supposed to be removed before you taxi. This day, in my haste, I had forgotten to remove them when I got into the jet.

My next down was due to my inability to smoothly control the power during landing approaches. I was "awarded" two additional flights to work on this deficiency. After the two flights, I had improved enough to be allowed to go to the Lex with my classmates. I carrier qualified after two attempts. The first one was from Beeville and then two weeks later a group of us flew to Pensacola where we finished up.

One thing I recall about the F-9 aircraft is that the tail hook was stowed inside the aircraft during routine flight. When you planned to land at the carrier, you had to ratchet it out of its stowed position through a hole below the engine exhaust. Then it would fall to its usual angled position for landing. If you wanted to raise it again, it would go to a position called a "stinger," but wouldn't go back into the stowed position in the aircraft again until you landed and the maintenance crew reset it using some sort of gadget to push it back inside the aircraft.

Wings of Gold

On May 14, I flew my last hop in the F-9, successfully finishing Advanced Jet Training. I was awarded my "Wings of Gold," becoming a member of an elite group of pilots called Naval Aviators. I had requested fleet assignment to F-4 Phantoms, but there were no F-4 seats available, so I was ordered to the East Coast A-7 Replacement Air Group or R.A.G. The A-7 was the Navy's newest jet aircraft in 1969 and I felt honored to be assigned to fly them.

LTjg Marty Herzog gets his Wings of Gold

Just think, sixteen months ago, I had never piloted an aircraft and now I was a qualified carrier jet Naval Aviator. What a trip! What a year! How could life get any better?

CHAPTER 4

A-7 TRAINING

May 1969 – March 1970

Events in the Navy and Worldwide During This Time
July 20, 1969   Apollo 11 Lunar module Eagle landed on the Moon and Neil Armstrong took his historic first steps. "That's one small step for man, one giant leap for mankind." August 15-18, 1969   Woodstock The Woodstock Festival was held in upstate New York.

Temporary Duty – N.A.S. Corpus Christi, Texas

Before reporting to the Replacement Air Group Squadron (The R.A.G.) to learn to fly A-7s, I was assigned a ten week temporary duty in Corpus Christi, Texas. The assignment was to fly R.O.T.C. midshipmen, who were on summer duty, to give them an opportunity to experience aviation. After their graduation, some of these midshipmen would eventually fly in the fleet.

There were no women pilots in the Navy in those days. These midshipmen were all young men. Upon reporting, they were fitted with flight suits, boots, and a helmet and sent to us for one flight each. The helmets were previously used by student pilots who had dropped from the flight program. They were often too big for the midshipmen's heads. Some of the looser fitting helmets could actually be spun around while the midshipman was wearing them. The helmet had speakers in the ear cups and a "lip" microphone, which were used for two way communication between the instructor and the student, while in flight. If the helmet was too big, the student's ears would be too far away from the speakers in the helmet and instructions from the instructor would be very difficult to understand.

Before flying the midshipmen, we (instructors) had two weeks to re-familiarize ourselves with our old friend, the T-34B "Mentor" – for most of us, it was the first plane that we ever flew. After flying jets, it seemed like a toy, so simple to fly.

One wonderful side note: there was no ground school. So on May 21, I flew my first T-34 re-familiarization flight.

After a few flights, we all felt very confident in the Mentor. Many of us tried a few things that weren't in the syllabus while training at Saufley Field over a year ago.

Formation:

We had to be a bit careful not to get too close since there was a propeller to deal with.

Air Combat Maneuvering:

T-34B Mentor in formation

Not normally done with a T-34. We decided that if we were one on one, turning in a high G circle, we wouldn't need to actually get behind the other aircraft. We were so close that if we were in combat we could open the canopy and shoot across the circle with a .45 pistol.

None of that mattered anyway, since the T-34 was a simple basic trainer and didn't have any armament.

Snap rolls:

> The T-34's normal aileron roll was very sluggish compared to the F-9 and T-2 aileron rolls, so when we found out about the snap roll, many of us wanted to try it. It was essentially a horizontal spin. You avoided spins in jets, but they were commonplace and quite safe in prop aircraft.
>
> There were basically three axes for control in an aircraft: Pitch (up and down, controlled by using forward or back stick), roll (to the left and right, controlled by using left and right stick), and yaw (nose to the left and right, controlled by using rudder pedals under the pilot's feet). To do a normal aileron roll, the pilot would pull the nose up about 10-15 degrees and push the stick full left or right. In a prop aircraft, the plane would slowly roll left or right until the pilot returned the stick to center. In a jet aircraft the roll rate was much faster, more responsive. We were used to that faster rate of roll.
>
> To do a snap roll, the pilot would slow the aircraft, retard the power and quickly pull the nose up and apply full rudder (left worked the best.) The aircraft would go into what's called an accelerated stall and would "depart" flight into a quick roll. The spin would end as soon as you returned the controls to neutral. One "small" problem was that these horizontal spins tended to put extra stress on the aircraft and could actually damage the airframe. Naively, we didn't think about that.

Soon the midshipmen showed up and the instructors were flying three fights each day: three midshipmen, one right after the other. We would brief each midshipman about what to do if there was an emergency, things he could touch and things he shouldn't touch in the airplane. We would give each midshipman an opaque plastic bag which was labeled "in case of air sickness" and would head out to the flight line. As we walked to the airplane, we would tell the midshipman some of the things we could do (if they wanted) during the flight: rolls, loops, barrel rolls, spins, etc. Some of the midshipmen would say, "I want to see it all," while others would say "straight and level and let's get this over with." We generally tried to comply with their requests.

Three stories come to mind, but first a little about the landing pattern. When approaching the field, the pilot (the midshipman), who was seated in the front cockpit, opened his canopy by releasing a latch and sliding the canopy backwards. The rear canopy stayed closed. We generally flew directly to the field at 1000 feet altitude, 120 knots, and entered the landing pattern. All three of these stories involve this approach to the landing pattern.

Story 1: Midshipman Jim's helmet was one of the "spinners" (very loose on his head). This helmet had no chin strap either. During the flight, Jim was doing pretty well and seemed to be enjoying himself. While coming back the field, after he opened the canopy, something under the aircraft caught his attention and he stretched over the canopy rail to see it. His head (and helmet) were actually partially outside of the aircraft. The airstream caught his helmet and ripped it off of his head. The last I saw of it, it was spiraling down toward some South Texas farmer's field. Jim was bare-headed and quite perplexed. I yelled up to him from the back seat to keep his head inside the aircraft. After landing, as we taxied back to the line, there were several "double- takes" as people looked at my aircraft. I'm sure it was very odd to see Jim seated in the front seat with no helmet. Jim's helmet was never recovered.

Story 2: Midshipman Ken was one of the "keep it straight and level" guys. However, he did want to try flying. I gave the controls to him once we got up to 3000 feet. He seemed to be doing OK but then he revealed to me that he felt sick. I took the controls and told him to get his airsickness bag out, just in case. He nodded and before too long I saw him leaning over in the front cockpit. I assumed he was filling the bag with his breakfast.

Pretty soon his head came back up. I had us on approach to the field. We were at 1000 feet, 120 knots. I told Ken to open the front canopy. He said "What?" "Open the canopy!" I said, louder this time. It's normally pretty hard to hear in the aircraft, but with the substandard helmets the mids had, it was even harder. He opened the canopy. Remembering the lost helmet flight, I told him, "Be careful with the bag. Don't let it get outside of the aircraft." He said, "What?" I said it again, "Don't let it outside the aircraft." He said, "Outside? Yes sir" and out it went. He threw his bag full of breakfast out of the aircraft. The slipstream brought it right back to the aircraft. Splat! Thank goodness my canopy was closed because that's exactly where it hit and streamed from there all the way back to the tail section. What a mess. Well, at least Ken had his helmet, but the aircraft needed a bath.

Story 3: Midshipman Matt was one of the "show me everything" guys. He was loving it. We had done loops, spins, rolls and he was clearly having the time of his life. He didn't know or understand a whole lot, but he was enjoying the experience. Coming back to the field at 1000 feet, 120 knots, Matt opened the canopy when requested. Everything was going fine when I asked him if he could see the field. He said no. I told him the field was at 1:00. Then Matt looked down at his watch, so I figured I should be more explicit. "The field is on your right -- up ahead. Do you see it?" He said, "I'm looking." Then he sat up straighter and said "There it is." He pointed at the field, extending his right hand out of the aircraft into the slipstream. Oh no, here we go again. If you have ever stuck your hand out of the window of an automobile going 60 miles per hour, you know what happened next. His hand immediately snapped backwards, his armpit on the canopy rail and his hand flapping back against the outside of my canopy. It took him nearly a minute to get his arm back into the cockpit.

The ten-week temporary assignment, a break from the rigors of training, was soon over and it was time to get on with learning about the A-7 Corsair II.

Corsair II – Jacksonville, Florida

Upon arriving in Jacksonville, I joined up with another student, Pete Leum, to share an apartment: The Normandy Apartments were located on Jammes Road near San Juan Avenue. Pete was a great roommate and quite a ladies' man. These apartments are still there but I believe they have a different name

Pete Leum – ladies' man

now. We were just a 25 minute drive away from the VA-174 (Attack Squadron One Seven Four) hangar.

After reporting to VA-174 at N.A.S. Cecil Field, our first assignment was ... ground school. We had to learn about the systems in the A-7 and tactics used to fly this awesome jet. Then we were sent to VA-45 (Attack Squadron Four Five) for instrument refresher training...10 more bag hops (instrument training) in the TA-4J Skyhawk. At least we were flying jets again. The A-7 was next, but not quite yet. We still had flight simulator training, which solidified our understanding of emergency procedures and gave us a feel for the jet.

Taxi Practice

I had reported to VA-174 in early August but didn't get to fly the A-7 until November 3. Before actually flying the A-7, we had to learn how to handle the aircraft on the ground. So, our first experience in the Corsair was a ground evolution. I pre- flighted the aircraft and then strapped in and did all of the checklists: pre-start checklist, start checklist and pre-taxi checklist. After starting the jet and doing the normal pre-taxi checks of equipment (flaps, launch bar, tail hook, etc.) I called Ground Control on the radio for permission to taxi to the duty runway. I taxied out of the line area, using nose wheel steering for the first time. (The T-34, T-2 and F-9 did not have nose wheel steering.) Nose wheel steering made turning so much easier to control.

After taxiing to the duty runway, I parked in the "Hold Short" area, did the take-off check list and then called the Tower for permission to taxi onto the duty runway for high speed roll out. After gaining that permission, I taxied onto the center line of the runway and pressed hard on the brakes (under my feet), and pushed the throttle forward to full power.

I felt the aircraft squat a little as I watched the instruments wind up to full power. I checked all of the engine gauges: RPM, EGT (exhaust gas temperature), oil pressure and several others. They all looked OK so I released the brakes and the A-7 started rolling down the runway. When the speed reached 80 knots, I throttled back to idle and pulled back gently on the stick to slightly rotate the aircraft – not fast enough to fly yet. And then started to gently apply the brakes. There was plenty of runway left to slow down and stop. So, I slowed to taxi speed and rolled to the end of the runway and turned off onto a taxiway. I switched the radio back to Ground Control and taxed back to line to shut down the aircraft.

Only One Seat in an A-7

There was only one seat in this aircraft. They hadn't built the two-seat model yet. So, my first flight was a solo! On the first few flights, an instructor pilot "chased" me. He was right there beside me in his jet for the entire flight. When

A-7 Corsair II with VA-93 markings

it was time to land, an L.S.O. (Landing Signal Officer) kept an eye on me from the end of the runway. After a few landings, my anxiety lessened and I said to myself, "I can really fly this plane." Back in the Ready Room after the flight, I met with the instructor and the L.S.O. who critiqued my flight and gave me some tips on how to improve. I flew another 11 flights in November before being sent to S.E.R.E. School.

S.E.R.E. School - Brunswick, Maine

On November 30, I was among a number of students in VA-174 who were airlifted to N.A.S. Brunswick, Maine for S.E.R.E. School (S.E.R.E. = Survival Evasion Resistance and Escape). This was a school to prepare us for the very real possibility of having to avoid being captured by the enemy after ejecting from our jet while in combat.

Day 1 and 2: Arrival and classroom training.

During the first two days, we were given classroom training about various aspects of S.E.R.E.: especially what to do and what not to do, should we be captured. We were also briefed on the rules of our upcoming field training.

Day 3: Field Training - Survival

After a two-hour bus ride to a remote location in Maine, we were greeted by some men whom we called "rangers."

They would be our instructors for the next two days. After two days, we would be on our own. The bus dropped us off at the foot of a mountain and the rangers told us to grab our gear.

We were going to take a hike. Each of us had about 40 pounds of gear to carry up a mountain road to our camp site. The trip took about an hour. They could have dropped us (and the gear) off at the camp site, but that wouldn't have been near as much fun.

When we got to the camp site, we were put in four groups of ten, each with a ranger, who gave us some more survival instruction, preparing us for the rigors of the next few days. Each team was assigned a wooden lean-to and given one live rabbit. The lean-to was our hotel and the rabbit was our dinner. One skinny rabbit for ten hungry men. That wasn't going to go too far. That afternoon, we managed to prepare and share our "rabbit stew," while warming ourselves by the fire.

Did I mention that this was December in Maine and the temperature was in the 20's and there was over a foot of snow on the ground around the campsite? We were issued parkas, boots, gloves and water repellant pants so we were able to keep somewhat warm, but we knew that the temperature was going to be much colder during the night. So, as it got dark, the ten of us, hungry and cold, squeezed into the lean-to to get what sleep we could as we anticipated the next day's activities.

Day 4 and 5 – Field Training - Evasion

The next morning, we were greeted by the rangers and given the plans for the day. We were going to travel by foot on a trail through the forest, with "enemy" forces nearby. If the enemy approached our column, we were to get off the trail and lie face down in or under the brush and wait for them to pass. We were not to try to overpower them since they would be well armed and we were not armed at all.

We were each given a tarp, a blanket, a compass, a rough map of the area, some rope and a can of C-rats. The C-rats (C-rations) was a survival package containing five crackers, some instant coffee, powdered milk and a packet of sugar. We folded the tarp and blanket into a kind of back-pack and tied it with the rope. We slung the packs on our backs and were on our way to the next camp site.

The rangers led us on the trail for a while and then told us to continue on the trail and that they would catch up with us in about an hour. About 15 minutes later, we heard some jeeps and some shooting. We dove into the brush and concealed ourselves as best as we could. Soon the enemy was coming down the trial, talking loudly in English, but with a Russian accent, calling each other "Comrade." When they got to our location, they slowed down and lingered right where we were, talking about how they were going to hurt the American intruders when they caught them. Everyone must have stayed still enough for them because after about 10 minutes, they left. Shortly thereafter, we heard the sound of jeeps leaving the area.

We got up and began moving again and were soon joined by the rangers who led us the rest of the way to our new camp site. They told us to remain within the boundaries of the campsite and find a way to conceal ourselves that night as we would probably be visited again by the enemy. Sure enough, we had another similar visit later that night.

In the morning we were joined once again by the rangers who gave us the instructions for the day. We would be completely on our own that day. They told us to navigate from where we were at the moment (Point A on our maps), to another location (point B) to the east, just north of an east/west road, which we were not allowed to cross. We were told that the enemy patrolled the road. If we got to point B without being captured, there would be a reward for us. Then we were to navigate to another location, point C. If we made it to point C, we would be given a hot meal. We were all hungry. A hot meal really sounded good. The area between B and C had more enemy forces in it and we would have to be much more careful about being spotted. If we were spotted and captured, we would be taken to a P.O.W. (prisoner of war) camp. At 5:00 PM, a siren would sound indicating that this phase was over.

When we heard the siren, we were supposed to head south down the mountain to the east/west road to be picked up and taken to the P.O.W. camp.

I paired up with another student pilot from VA-174 and we decided to go halfway up the mountain, even though we knew the snow would be deeper up there. Then we would head east and down to point B. We did that, but it took quite a long time. It was really hard trudging through the three-foot deep snow on the side of the mountain. When we finally got to point B, we were given a Styrofoam cup of hot chocolate (our reward for making it to point B). Hot chocolate never tasted so good.

Day 5 Night: Capture

Getting to point C never happened for my friend and me, since we had lost too much time getting from A to B. When the siren sounded, we came down the mountain to the road and were picked up in a jeep and taken to the P.O.W. Camp where our equipment was taken from us and we were processed in as "war criminals." We were each given a round disk with a number on one side and nothing on the other side, which we wore on a string around our necks. We were told that the number must always be visible to the guards. If they couldn't see your number, they might smack you around some.

Day 6 and 7: P.O.W. Camp

The P.O.W. camp was surrounded by a fence, with only one gate that I could see, large enough to drive a bus through. There was a guard tower and a few buildings next to the gate and snow-covered trees outside the fence on three sides. The buildings, we assumed, were the guards' quarters.

Inside the fence, there were a few more crude buildings. These were P.O.W. "quarters." There was nothing inside any the buildings that I was able to access – just four walls. We were allowed to use these buildings to get a few hours (two – three hours) sleep during the night.

The rangers had told us that if we managed to escape from the P.O.W. camp, we would be given a hot meal, and then returned to the camp after one hour. Also, if someone escaped, there would be reprisals for the rest of the prisoners. Prior to leaving camp for point A on Day Five all of the students agreed, that if someone thought they could escape, they should try it. Don't worry about any reprisals to the rest of us. Get out if you can.

One black enlisted guy escaped twice. I'm not sure how he did it, but after two escapes, he was punished rather severely. He was brought out into the middle of the camp area and stripped down to only his undershorts and told to stand there. After about 30 minutes his skin had begun to turn white from the cold. The air temperature was in the 20's (degrees Fahrenheit).

The American senior officer went to the guards to ask that they let the enlisted man come into the building to warm up. The guards refused and took the senior officer in for interrogation. We never saw him again until the training was over.

Now the Number 2 man was in charge. He also went to the guards on behalf of the black man who appeared to be nearing hypothermia. That was it for Number 2. However, the black guy was taken into the guard's building, we assumed for medical care.

We all started checking among ourselves to see who was senior among those of us still remaining. I was a Lieutenant, junior grade. I didn't feel that I was very senior, but I was horrified to find out that I was Number 7.

Number 3 was taken away next, leaving Number 4 in charge. Then my number was called to go in for interrogation. Wait! I'm not next…Number 4 is next. I failed to realize that everyone was getting interrogated – not just the senior guys. I went to the gate, showed my number to the guard and was none too gently escorted to a room with no windows.

At this point, I tried to recall the information we were given on day one and two. We were told that the Geneva Convention only required

74

us to give our name, rank, serial number and date of birth to the enemy and that we should not be tortured for withholding other information. We were also told that many countries such as Vietnam did not sign the Geneva Convention Pact, so we shouldn't expect them to honor it. They would most likely use torture to get information from us. If we were tortured, we should only give information as necessary to save our lives. Actually, we really knew very little that the enemy didn't know already. Our statements would most likely be used for propaganda purposes.

Once in the interrogation room, a very nice guard gestured for me to sit down and asked me if I wanted a cigarette. I was a smoker and hadn't had a cigarette for over 12 hours, so I took it, hoping to allow this moment linger for a while. After getting my name, rank, serial number and date of birth, this guard said he didn't care to hear me tell him that information again. Then he started asking me questions: "What kind of aircraft did you fly?", "Do you agree with America's policy about invading Vietnam?" "Do you understand why your president has sent you here to kill innocent Vietnamese people?" I don't think I did a very good job deflecting these questions, but wanted to savor the cigarette. Soon this interrogation was over and I was escorted to another larger room.

There were six wooden boxes on the floor of this room and three smaller rooms to the side. These smaller rooms were about 4 feet wide and 6 feet long. As I was brought in, one of the other prisoners was being "stuffed" into one of the boxes. The boxes were about 2 ½ feet wide, 3 feet long and 3 feet high. The prisoner was told to kneel down in the box and then his head was pushed down and a hinged door was swung over the top of the box and locked. "Oh no," I thought "I'm next."

I was taken through the door of one of the small rooms and told to put my hands on one wall and my feet four feet away against the other wall, leaning across the room. As I turned to enter the room, I noticed a wet crumpled American flag on the floor. Careful not to step on it, I positioned myself as instructed. I was directly over the flag and soon I noticed the smell of urine rising up from it. I started to get angry. That was probably what they hoped for.

After about ten minutes in this position, a guard came in and began to question me. He had a cigar and a long tube. He held the tube up to my nose and blew cigar smoke through the tube into my face. Ha! You can't hurt me with that. I'm a smoker. After a while he gave that up and started asking questions and slapping me when he didn't like my answers, then a few punches...nothing unbearable, but I had to work at keeping calm. I knew if I struck back at him, I would get clobbered.

He did the smoke and slapping routine for about 20 minutes and appeared to get tired of that and told the other guards to "Box him!" and into one of the boxes I went. During high school, I went on several spelunking trips, cave exploring. So, I knew I was not claustrophobic. Being closed in, in one of those boxes, wouldn't be a problem for me. I was ready for the box and managed to position myself below the lid before they slammed it closed and locked it. They took turns kicking the sides of the boxes to be sure we stayed awake. I managed a few cat-naps. We were all pretty sleepy by now. We hadn't slept much the past few nights.

An hour later, I was back in the prison yard with the rest of the group, having survived my interrogations. I noticed Number 4 had been taken away. I was told that the guards had instructed him to have the prisoners fall in. They brought out an enemy flag and told Number 4 to have the prisoners salute it. He refused and was taken away. Number 5 was now in charge. He was a junior Lieutenant. Then it would be number 6, a Lieutenant, junior grade like me and then number 7 – me.

Day 7 Night – Rescue

In the back of all of our minds, we knew this was training, but it seemed pretty real. We all wondered when it would end. It had been miserable! About an hour after the sun had set while we were contemplating another night in the camp, we were rescued.

The guards had called us out to line up in formation and had just taken the attendance report from Number 5, when the gates burst open and a jeep drove in at high speed with the rangers. One was holding an American flag. That was all we needed. The tension and restraint that we had forced on ourselves over the past few days was released. We exploded and charged the guards as they took off for the guard buildings. Then the loud speakers, that had been playing this irritating oriental music for the entire time we were there, started playing the National Anthem. The rangers held their hands up to stop us and we knew the "game" was over. We all stopped and saluted the flag that the rangers had brought in while the music played. After it was over, we were instructed to load into a bus for the trip back to Brunswick.

Relieved, tired, sore and hungry, we boarded the bus for the long trip back to the base. We got back some time after midnight and were taken to the galley. We hadn't eaten much of anything for the past four days. The cooks were waiting for us and cooked us whatever breakfast items we wanted. We lined up and made our orders, not realizing that our stomachs had shrunk over the past few days. Most of us ordered more than we could eat. Exhausted, but pleasantly full we headed to our quarters for some well-deserved sleep.

Day 8 – Debrief

I woke up the next morning with a sore throat. I imagine that was because nothing much had gone down it for four days until we ate our breakfast the previous night.

After a group debriefing, we were individually debriefed – told what we did right and wrong during the field training. Our senior officer (Number 1) was there. His arm was bandaged and he was limping a little, but he was all smiles. We realized that he had taken some real abuse, much more than any of the rest of us. He told us that his training was very meaningful and that his treatment, if he were to be captured by a real enemy, would be much worse.

Then it was over. That evening, most of us went into town to get a Maine lobster dinner and to celebrate completion of this school, hoping that we would never have to do it again. We had a good time joking amongst ourselves that we had just received our survival training for Vietnam, a jungle area, by trudging through three feet of snow for a week.

Day 9 – Jacksonville

The next day, while walking out to the aircraft that was waiting to take us back to Jacksonville, we passed about 40 guys that we assumed were the incoming class. I was so happy to be finished and felt a bit sorry for them. A cold front had passed through the night before and dumped another 8-12 inches of snow in the mountains.

We flew back to Jacksonville and were granted several weeks of Christmas leave. After what was the most intense training I had ever received and the most unpleasant school I had ever participated in, I was grateful for some time off.

More Flight Training

One of the first flights I had upon returning from Christmas leave was with Commander Marv Reynolds (XO of VA-174 at that time; XO = Executive Officer, second in command). He taught me one of the most valuable lessons I had while training in the A-7. It was how to fly your aircraft right up to the edge of an accelerated stall without "crossing the line" and actually stalling. For the layman, that's hard to understand. An accelerated stall occurs when an aircraft departs flight due to high G loading.

We were practicing some air to air combat maneuvering and I was behind his aircraft tracking him in my gun sight in a high G left hand turn. My aircraft was buffeting slightly. I knew that buffeting occurred when your aircraft was close to stalling. Commander Reynolds prompted me to pull just a little harder to get inside the turn. As soon as I did that, my aircraft "departed" flight and rolled uncontrollably to the right. XO said on the radio, "OK, you have just departed. Just let go of the stick and you will recover." As soon as I eased the pull (and therefore the G loading), the aircraft began acting normal again, responding to normal stick movements.

Of course, had this been an actual combat situation, I would have lost my advantage and might have been shot down by the enemy aircraft. I had learned the boundary between buffet flying and departure. A very important lesson, since departure from flight is not a good thing in combat. I found out later that he was known for this lesson. One of my friends told me, "Yeah, he did that to me, too."

Electrical Failure

One of the most important phases of training in the A-7 was night air-to-ground weapons delivery. Normally a flight of four A-7s would fly to Pinecastle Bombing Range and upon arrival, we would fly over the target at an altitude of 5,000 feet. At timed intervals, each individual jet would, in turn, go to full power and peel off to the left and fly a full circle to a roll-in position at 10,000 feet. This maneuver set up a circular pattern with the jets about 15 seconds apart.

As each pilot approached the roll-in point, he would roll his aircraft to a somewhat inverted position to pull his plane's nose down to the target. He would then roll out, adjusting his power and dive angle to arrive at the drop point of 5,000 feet at 450 knots and 30 degrees of dive. At that point, the pilot would pickle his bomb(s) and pull up, return to full power, roll left to turn back to the roll in point.

Even though this was visual bombing, it was all done in the darkness of night. The pilot's scan included items inside and outside of the cockpit: altitude, airspeed, attitude, and obviously the target, which was usually a small fire on the ground, as well as keeping an eye on the other three aircraft in the pattern.

One night, I was flying in a division of four A-7s in this bombing pattern at Pinecastle and while I was in the middle of rolling my jet in on the target, nearly inverted, my trusty A-7 had a complete electrical failure. All my interior and exterior lights went out and all my instruments failed. My navigation equipment and radios – all inoperative. Me and my jet with no electrical power, in the dark night pointed at the ground – inverted. As a note, the engine doesn't need electricity to run. So, it was working fine. I just couldn't monitor it.

Fortunately, there was a pretty good horizon that night since there was a half-moon in the sky. Also, I had 10,000 feet of altitude. I was able to quickly right my A-7, keep flying and get the nose up into a climb. Then I deployed the R.A.T. (Ram Air Turbine). The R.A.T. was a generator, stored in a compartment on the right side of the plane. When deployed, the compartment opened and the turbine rotated out into the airstream attached to a hinged door. It was essentially a propeller that spun in the air to produce electricity.

The R.A.T. produced emergency electricity to only the most essential items in the aircraft. (radio, attitude gyro, flaps and some engine and navigation instruments) I was now able to inform my flight leader of my dilemma. He told me that if I felt safe, I should orbit the target above 12,000 feet, keeping the flight in sight while they completed their mission. My heart rate soon returned to normal and when everyone was finished, we joined up safely and returned to Cecil Field for an uneventful landing.

Weapons and Carrier Landings

At the end of January, I was sent, along with about 15 other students, to Marine Corps Air Station, Yuma, Arizona for a weapons detachment. The weather in Arizona was perfect this time of year, while in Jacksonville it was often rainy and many weapons flights were cancelled. Not in Yuma. We were flying twice a day, for 3 weeks. After 2 weeks, the L.S.O.s from VA-174 flew out to begin our F.C.L.P.s (Field Carrier Landing Practice), our training for landing the A-7 on a carrier.

A week later, we returned to Cecil Field to finish our carrier training…more F.C.L.P.s (day and night) and then a trip to *U.S.S. Intrepid* (CVS-11) for Carrier Qualification.

I was told that the catapult on *Intrepid* was different from *Lexington's*. The catapult was a system on the ship designed to propel the aircraft down 150 feet of flight deck accelerating the aircraft to flying speed. All the pilot would have to do is keep his throttle at 100% and rotate the jet slightly when it reached the end of its run. *Lexington* had steam catapults, but we were told that *Intrepid* had hydraulic "cats." A steam catapult would gradually increase the speed of the jet from 0 to about 150 knots over the 150 foot run while a hydraulic "cat" gave you flying speed almost instantaneously. It was more of a jolt. I was not experienced enough to be able to tell the difference.

After 12 day traps (carrier landings) over a period of three days, it was time for night traps. Day traps are actually fun and most carrier aviators love them. However, night traps are quite different. During approach on a dark night, there was no horizon and no visual cues as to your aircraft's attitude. Were you level, turning, rolling? You couldn't tell without keeping your head "in the cockpit" and on the gauges. It took much more attention. But you had to have your eyes outside the cockpit as well. There were other aircraft out there.

Then, there was the possibility of vertigo. Most every pilot has experienced vertigo at one time or another. Physiologically, the fluid in your inner ear helps you keep balanced, but can be misleading at times. For example, if you close your eyes and spin one way on a swivel chair, and all of a sudden stop, your ears will be telling your brain that you are now spinning the other way, even though you are stopped. As soon as you open your eyes and see your surroundings, that sensation goes away. In a sense, your eyes override your ears.

On an approach at night, often your eyes cannot see a horizon, so it's like they were closed and now your ears are in charge. So, your ears can fool you into believing you are turning when you are not or climbing when you are actually descending. A pilot MUST depend on and trust what his cockpit instruments are telling him and fight the tendency to believe what he feels.

I was a bit nervous about my first night landings and mercifully, my first night trap was scheduled as a "pinkie." Launch came right at sunset. So, it wasn't really dark yet, and as I climbed to altitude, the sky became even brighter. But the sky darkened again as soon as I started descending to land. But even so, it wasn't completely black. I got four traps that night – the second, third and fourth were in the pitch-black night, as were my next four night traps the following night.

On March 9, my training with VA-174 was complete and I was ready for assignment to my fleet squadron. It was then that I found out about several things that had happened during the last few weeks. I was originally scheduled to be an "East Coast" pilot, but in February, a pilot from a West Coast squadron, assigned to *U.S.S. Ranger*, had died in an aircraft crash. That squadron was now undermanned and needed a replacement quickly. Since I had nearly finished my training, I was assigned to be that pilot.

My training could have been stretched out for an additional 3-4 weeks, but because the fleet needed a pilot right away, I became a "must pump," a pilot who was given priority on flights and was scheduled two flights each day to get him completed as soon as safely possible.

To see how this worked in my case, I was scheduled for only 12 flights during November and December, but from January 7 through March 9, I flew 45 flights. I was detached from VA-174 on the day that I flew my last training flight…March 9. My orders were to proceed and report to VA-93 on *U.S.S. Ranger* (CVA-61) at whatever port *U.S.S. Ranger* was in. But first I had to check out through medical. They checked my shot record and poked me with 4-5 needles with various vaccines and preventatives in case I would have to eject over the South China Sea.

One of these shots was called a "Gee-Gee" (Gamma- Globulin). When I saw the corpsman holding the needle, my eyeballs nearly bugged out. There was so much fluid in the tube, it looked like you should drink it. Where was he going to stick that thing? He told me that it was going to be injected in my buttocks. "All of it?" I asked, shocked that he was seriously going to try to put all of that serum in my posterior. He said, "I can put half on the left side and the other half on the right, but that would be two hurts instead of one. What would you like?" I took the "one hurt option" and had to sit side-saddle for two days afterward.

After that, I was granted a week of leave and was soon on my way to California to catch a M.A.C. flight to Japan. (M.A.C. = Military Air Command – which is like the military's airline service) My training was over and now it was time for me to report to my combat squadron. While I dreaded the idea of combat flying and being shot at, I realized that after nearly two years of training, it was now time to join the fleet and pay my dues.

CHAPTER 5

U.S.S. RANGER CRUISE

March 1970 – March 1971

Events in the Navy and worldwide during this time

November 17, 1970   Vietnam War
Lieutenant William Calley went on trial for the My Lai massacre.

November 19, 1970
Commander Dave Glunt relieved by Commander Rudy Kohn as Commanding Officer of VA-93 (NAS Lemoore, California)

January 31, 1971   Apollo program
Apollo 14 (Alan Shepard, Stuart Roosa, and Edgar Mitchell) lifted off on the third successful lunar landing mission.

Japan

Finally, I was on my way to WestPac. (Western Pacific) … to my fleet squadron - VA-93 (Attack Squadron Nine Three) onboard *U.S.S. Ranger.* When I reported to Military Airlift Command at Travis Air Force Base (northeast of San Francisco), I didn't know what to expect.

I had put my Fiat in storage in San Francisco, as well as my other belongings except for what I could fit in my duffel bag. That had to include my flight gear and uniforms. There wasn't a whole lot of room for much else.

My orders said to report to Travis, but what then? How do I find *Ranger*? Where is she? Somebody must know. Sure enough, when I checked in with my orders, they quickly had me booked to Tokyo, Japan. The booking was quick but I had to wait a few days before actually leaving. So, after a couple of days in San Francisco, I was on my way to Japan.

The first leg of my journey took me to Anchorage, Alaska. Then after another delay, I was off to Japan. When I reached Yokota Air Base in Tokyo, I was told how to get to where *Ranger* was. The long trip to Sasebo took nearly 18 hours by bus. Once there, it was easy to find *Ranger*. After coming aboard the fore-brow of *Ranger*, I was escorted to the VA-93 Ready Room and eventually to the stateroom which I shared with LT(jg) Tom Laakso.

VA93 squadron patch

So finally, after two and half years of training, I was in my fleet squadron. I found out that Tom was the roommate of Rick Stevenson, the pilot who had died and who I had been sent to replace. That meant that I was sleeping in Rick's rack ... just a bit unnerving.

When we got underway from Japan, we had two days of training on the way to Yankee Station. (Yankee Station is a region in the northern Gulf of Tonkin where aircraft carriers position themselves for combat operations in North and South Vietnam.) At this time, we weren't bombing North Vietnam, so I imagine we were positioned somewhat south of the usual Yankee Station.

Climbing into my A7

Bad Weather

My first flights were with the skipper (a commanding officer was affectionately known as "Skipper"), Commander Dave Glunt. A squadron skipper often wants to fly with the new guys just so he can personally observe how they handle themselves. That was me – the new guy (The veterans called the new guys nuggets). I was the "nugget." The skipper would continue to fly with a nugget until he felt comfortable about him.

Upon returning to the ship at the end of my first flight, I was told to do 2 touch and goes before lowering my tail hook. (Touch and goes were landings with the tail hook up, followed by going to full power and taking off again.) I guess they wanted to be sure I was safe before allowing me to land. No problem.

My second flight was supposed to be an intercept with the Taiwanese Air Force. We flew our track, but they never showed up. Oh well. "Back Ship" for landing and dinner. When we switched to tower frequency, we were told the ship was in heavy thunderstorms. We should contact "Marshall Control" for landing instructions.

Marshal Control told us that the weather at the ship was nearing minimums, and we should enter a holding pattern until the ship was ready for us. The skipper and I were each given our individual approach times and holding instructions. The skipper lowered his tail hook and "kissed me off" to go to my holding location. "Kissing off" is a gesture like throwing a kiss which means that the second aircraft should leave to fly on his own.

I lowered my hook also and turned away from the skipper and climbed to my holding location. At the appropriate time I "pushed over" to begin my approach for landing, reporting to Marshal Control, "Raven 301, leaving marshal, state 3.5." The state was how much fuel remained in the aircraft. 3.5 meant that I had 3,500 pounds of gas left. Plenty.

The holding pattern hadn't been too bad. I had been able to see just fine, but when I left Marshal, I was almost immediately in thick clouds. I had to completely depend on my instruments as I was trained to do.

The approach was radar controlled by a controller aboard *Ranger* who directed me to a point behind the ship on landing heading at 1200 feet. I was flying at approach speed at this point. All of that was fine, but I was still in the thick clouds and heavy rain. I couldn't see a thing. I began to get a little nervous.

It was time to begin my final descent, so I pulled back on the power, adjusted my nose and rate of descent, and pushed a little power back on, establishing my A-7 on the glide path. When I "broke out" of the clouds, I wanted to be in a good position to visually land the jet. I continued my descent, and the controller (on the ship) said "301, you're at 3/4 mile, call the ball." Even though I was intensely focused on my instruments, I had been sneaking peeks outside every five seconds or so. I looked up now, since I was 250 feet above the sea and coming down. The clouds were still thick and the rain was still heavy. I couldn't see anything ahead of me. On the radio, I declared "Clara."

"Clara" is the word a pilot uses when he cannot see the "ball" – his visual reference to the glide slope. I strained to see that yellow ball in between the green datum lights, but I couldn't. I couldn't see anything. The L.S.O. (Landing Signal Officer - on the ship) said "I've got you, keep it coming." How can he see me? I can't see him. Where is the ship? I can't see it! All I could see was the rain beating on my windscreen.

What if I hit something? Finally, the L.S.O. said "Wave it off" – that meant apply full power and climb. No argument from me. I was at 100 feet and still didn't see anything. Then all of a sudden, I saw the island of the ship pass by me on the right. I never saw it in front of me. I only saw streams of water beating on my windscreen.

The L.S.O. (who I found out later was Lieutenant Pete Nichols) said, "Hey, Marty, when you get a chance, make sure your rain removal is on." He knew who I was. At least he didn't say "Hey, Nugget. Get your act together." It was nice to hear a friendly voice with excellent advice. When I finished my climb to 1200 feet of altitude, I looked around on a panel way back on the left side by my hip and found the rain removal switch and turned it "ON." I had to turn in my seat somewhat to locate it. Why did they put such an important switch in such an awkward place? I guess pilots didn't use it very much.

I could hear the rain removal air blowing on the outside of my windscreen from a point outside, low and in front of the glass panel. As soon as I turned my rain removal on, the windscreen cleared up. It was still raining and I was still in the clouds, but my windscreen was clear. "Now if I can just land this thing," I thought to myself. My heart was pounding. My head was sweating, as well as just about every other part of me. But my focus was on the instrument panel. Now another trip around the pattern in the clouds.

I was told to turn to a heading that paralleled the ship in the opposite direction ("downwind"), so that I would be in good place to turn again to intercept the final bearing and descend to land.

As I rolled out heading downwind, I was at 1200 feet with my landing gear and flaps down "in the clag" (in the clouds with no visual ground reference). Then it hit me! -- Vertigo.

My head was telling me that I was in a right turn but my instruments were telling me that my wings were level. Then a burst of lightning off to my right somewhere added to my disorientation.

I wanted to push the stick left to roll out of the right turn, but my mind said "Look at your instruments". You are in level flight. This was a fight that I had to win. I continued to battle with my senses as the controller on the ship turned me to the left to parallel the ship and eventually intercept the final landing bearing. I reported, "301, Trouble City." That was a code telling the controller and everyone else that I was having difficulty. I was experiencing vertigo. Being aware of that, they were to give me only gentle, necessary turns and altitude changes – to watch me a little more closely.

After another few minutes, I was on glide slope, descending to land, but still in heavy weather. Then, mercifully, I "broke out" of the clouds at 300 feet. My vertigo instantly went away as I saw the ship. "301, ball, 2.9." This meant I saw the ball and had 2900 pounds of fuel. I was able to land safely this time. After taxiing forward very carefully in the pouring rain, my jet was tied down and it was over. Time to go to the ready room and face the music. I had blown it by not having the rain removal on.

In the ready room, the skipper slapped me on the back. Smiling at me he said, "That was some weather, wasn't it?" Our L.S.O., Pete Nichols debriefed me later. "Welcome to the fleet, Marty," he smiled. He was very encouraging during his debrief of my approaches, even though my approaches and their grades weren't great. But the bottom line was the nugget did OK. Not a word about rain removal, but I knew that they knew. I thought I heard the skipper say, "He (referring to the nugget - me) earned his spurs today." I have never forgotten to use rain removal on a rainy approach since that day...Never.

Combat

I must have passed the skipper's test because my next flight (my first combat flight) was with Lieutenant Commander Dave Rogers. I was sweating before we even began to brief. I was going to go out there to let people shoot at me! What if they hit me? Dave began the brief with the normal routine items that are discussed on every flight: rendezvous, radio frequencies, and emergency procedures. Then he recognized my anxiety and calmly discussed what I should to do if he were shot down, which I realized is exactly what he was going to do for me if I were shot down. We talked about ejection sequence, low level and high level, what radio frequencies to use for S.A.R. (S.A.R. = Search and Rescue), evasion techniques, etc. Then it was time to man our aircraft. I was still pretty anxious, but off we went. Four hours later, my first mission was complete. The nugget was now a veteran. Well, sort of. Well, maybe not a veteran. Not yet, but I had one combat mission under my belt.

There were several unusual events that happened during that month "on the line" ("On the line" means being on Yankee Station – or Dixie Station – flying combat missions).

Sidewinders and 20 mm Guns

The A-7 had 8 weapons stations and two 20 mm (millimeter) cannons that could be loaded with 250 rounds each. The stations were numbered from left to right with 4 and 5 being on the fuselage. Those

88

two stations were designed to carry air to air AIM 9 Sidewinder missiles. The A-7 was not a fighter. It was a bomber but having a Sidewinder with you gave you some sort of comfort in a MIG environment. (A MIG was an enemy fighter aircraft.)

On one of my early missions, I was flying with a Lieutenant Commander in the squadron. I will refer to him only as Raven 1, rather than use his name. Our aircraft were each carrying a Sidewinder in addition to the 12 Mark-82s (500 pound bombs) we were to use on the mission. We also had our 20 mm cannons loaded.

Our mission took us into Laos where we worked with a F.A.C. (F.A.C. = Forward Air Controller). F.A.C.s flew OV-10 aircraft and were very familiar with the area they were patrolling. As we passed over the coast of South Vietnam, we each heard some electronic sounds in our headset (buzzes and chirps) that indicated possible MIG activity nearby. Raven 1 called to me to be sure my Sidewinder missile was selected on my weapons panel. I turned the number 4 station switch to "ON." Now all I had to do was turn on the "Master Arm" switch and pull the trigger and the missile would fire.

We contacted the F.A.C., call sign Nail 31. He told us to meet him at a point inside Laos. Our target would be a suspected truck park (a hidden area where trucks might be parked during the day). Nail 31 marked the target with a "willy pete" smoke. He told us to put our bombs in an east to west line starting at his smoke. We worked with him on the target, rolling in one at a time, dropping our bombs in the jungle, two at a time. Although he thought there had been activity in that area, our bombs didn't produce any secondary explosions. As we were rejoining after dropping our weapons, Nail 31 told us that our weapons were 100% on target with no visual results. After the mission was complete, we headed back to the coast.

On the way back, we were called by F.A.C. Control to contact another F.A.C. in South Vietnam for close air support using our 20 mm. Twenty-millimeter rounds (we often called these rounds "20 mike mike") were fired like bullets, straight forward from two cannons in our aircraft. This action is called strafing. We switched over, contacted our new F.A.C. (Covey 05) and were briefed on the new target. Our new target was located inside a tree line that ran north-south. The F.A.C. shot a "willy-pete" smoke rocket where he wanted us to strafe. We were to shoot our 20 mm to the west of the line (in the trees). "Your target is 25 meters west of my smoke" the F.A.C. said. Raven 1 acknowledged the target and said he had it in sight and was rolling in. I was to wait until Raven 1 called "off" before I rolled in behind him. Raven 1 called, "Raven 1's in hot" which meant his master arm switch was on and he was rolling in to attack the target.

I was watching him to be sure I knew where the target was, when "whoosh" - a missile fired from his aircraft. Oh no. He fired his Sidewinder. He had forgotten to deselect his missile and when he pressed the trigger his guns and his missile both fired.

The F.A.C. got real excited. "Wow, Raven 1. That was GREAT! Two, have you got one of those also? Put yours just to the north of One's." -- "Ahhh no. I only have 20 mike mike," I said, while checking to be sure my Sidewinder was not selected. "Two's in, hot." Thinking to myself "but only with guns."

We all have to eat a little humble pie, now and then. That's kind of hard for pilots. I was remembering just a few days back to my rain removal incident and thought, "I'm not going to say anything about this." I knew he would have to do some explaining, but not to me. I was still the nugget.

A.C.M. over Vietnam?

During my first few weeks in VA-93, I flew over 20 combat missions. I was nowhere near the experience level of the other pilots in the squadron, but I was gaining experience. After one mission, working with a F.A.C. in Laos, I was returning to the ship with my fight lead, who I will call Big Dan (not his real name). Big Dan, unfortunately, had a rather poor reputation with the other pilots in the squadron.

As we were flying out of Laos into South Vietnam, he told me to take separation for A.C.M. (Air Combat Maneuvering). As I said, I was not very experienced, but I had enough brains to know we were still in a "threat environment" and in a busy traffic zone – not a good place to practice A.C.M. I told Big Dan, "Negative – unable." Shortly after crossing the coast into the relative safety of the Gulf of Tonkin, I made another radio call to my flight lead, that my issue had been corrected and I could now take that separation and do our one on one fight. What was he thinking?

Navy Showers

When at sea (underway) on an aircraft carrier, everyone on board is responsible for conserving fresh water. Fresh water is made by the ship's condensers and is used for normal things, such as food preparation, cleaning dishes, showering, washing, drinking, etc. but the biggest consumption is from the steam catapults, used to "shoot" (or launch) the air wing aircraft into the air. This mission capability is a major priority. The ship must maintain enough water to launch all mission aircraft during normal flight operations.

All hands are ordered to take what are called "Navy showers." A Navy shower procedure is as follows: Step in the shower stall, turn the water on to wet your body, then turn it off. Soap down, wash and then turn the water on to rinse and then turn it off again, using a minimum amount of water. -- A Navy shower. The normal way of showering where you leave the water on the entire time is known as a "hotel shower."

Sometimes when the water reserves on the ship are low, the ship will go on "water hours," which means the fresh water is turned off throughout the ship at some specified published time, normally for a few hours to allow the fresh water level to rise.

One night, I was showering. -- yes --- a Navy shower. I had wet my body, turned off the water and soaped down. Then I turned on the water nozzle to rinse off and a little trickle of water came out and then stopped altogether. Oh no! I had totally forgotten that the ship was starting a water hours cycle.

Now I had to figure out how to get the soap off of me. I went from shower to shower (six in all) and turned each one on to get the trickle of water that was still trapped in the pipes to rinse with. That wasn't really enough. Wait! What about the sinks? There were 8 sinks. Each had a minuscule amount of water trapped, which I gathered and used.

I dried and returned to my stateroom, promising myself that I would remember when the ship was going on water hours in the future and schedule my showers accordingly.

A New Tailhook for A–7s

Lieutenant Commander J.J. Fleming was the operations officer for VA-93. He had red hair and the kind of fiery temper that you often associate with red-heads. Toward the end of the "line period," he and I had just finished a mission together. He was ahead of me in the landing pattern. He made his landing approach but the flight deck wasn't ready, so he was "waved off." He had to climb back to 600 feet turn left to circle downwind and make another approach. So, I landed first and was taxiing forward to have my aircraft tied down. After being securely tied down, I was about to shut down the engine when I heard, "Boom!" I looked to my left and saw J.J.'s aircraft roll over the edge of the ship and him in an orange and white parachute about 100 feet in the air. He had just ejected. What happened? Why did he eject? Why did his aircraft go over the side of the ship?

I found out later that his tail hook had caught an arresting wire and pulled it out, slowing the aircraft down, but then the tail hook "spit" the wire. It just let the wire go after it had slowed his jet down. At that point, the aircraft was too slow to take off again and too fast to apply brakes and stop. Over the side it went. As soon as the nose wheel went over the edge, J.J. "punched out" (ejected). He landed in the water to the left of the ship and was almost immediately picked up by the rescue helicopter. This accident resulted in a redesign of the A-7 tail hook. This new design provided A-7 tail hooks that were longer and pointier.

Olongapo

On May 12th, the *Ranger's* last line period was over and we headed for Cubi Point, Philippines so that the ship could refuel and replenish for our trip home to California. While that was happening, the crew was granted some free time for R&R. Cubi Point, or more appropriately Naval Air Station, Cubi Point, was the

View of USS Ranger from Cubi Point Officers Club

closest port to Yankee Station and the one most often used for liberty between the line periods of a combat cruise to Vietnam. There was a lot to do there: movies, golf, bowling, swimming and more. Cubi had a wonderful Officer's Club on the top of a hill overlooking Subic Bay. What a view! Then there was the "Chuck Wagon," which had the best steaks in the Philippines. I had never been to any of these places, but I had heard about them and was looking forward to seeing all of them.

I was told that I should try going into town, not so much for food, but for entertainment. So, on my second night of liberty in the P.I. (Philippine Islands), I took the bus to "the gate" and exited the base. Outside the gate, I was instantly hit with the putrid smell of the Olongapo River.

The Po River (Olongapo River) smelled like sewage. I was pretty sure that much of the Olongapo sewage ended up in this river. Coming up to the bridge that passed over the Po River, I looked over to the side and saw scores of children in little canoes with baskets and other catching apparatus that they could use to snatch any offerings that the sailors might have for them. I noticed that if they couldn't catch the coins that were tossed or thrown, they would dive in the filthy water to try to retrieve them. My squadron mates told me not to give them coins but to keep my hands in my pockets, because there were thieves everywhere.

Looking ahead to the other side of the bridge I could see what appeared to be a scene from the "Wild West." Everyone seemed to have a gun. There were uniformed men and some not in uniforms, but all with guns: shotguns, pistols, submachine guns and rifles. There was an incredible mixture of sound coming from the buildings on both sides of the dirt and gravel road that went down the middle of town: all kinds and genres of music coming from all directions, people shouting and vendors selling their wares.

One of the items for sale along the road was "monkey on a stick." This was a piece of meat wrapped around a thin stick and cooked on a hibachi grill. These, I am told, were pretty good. Another item for sale was a balut (pronounced buh – loot). These are developing duck or chicken embryos, still in the shell, boiled and eaten out of the shell. They are considered a delicacy in the orient but not for me. No thanks.

Some of my squadron mates wanted me to go to a well-known bar on the east side of town, but others told me that I would be wise to not go, so I didn't. I found out later that this particular bar was known for live shows, gambling, sex, live music, and fights. Also, there was a live alligator in a pen in front of the building. The local children would sell baby ducklings to passers-by to feed to the gator.

Along the main road there were wall-to-wall bars, each with its own music and a bouncer carrying some kind of weapon. These bouncers were there to protect the bar and its patrons. But even so, the weapons seemed a bit intimidating. What a place! After only one night in Olongapo, I was ready to go home.

Home after the Cruise

After we got back to the good ole USA and had our post-cruise leave period, it was time to begin training for our next cruise. Several of the veteran pilots were "rotated out" to their next assignment, which in many cases involved flying in the training command. For each pilot that left, another new pilot reported in so we ended up with the same number. Also, in November 1970, Commander Dave Glunt was relieved by Commander Rudy Kohn. Many changes.

Tailhook Convention

During the summer of 1970, a number of us went to the annual Tailhook Convention in Las Vegas. This was a four day event held for Tailhookers and others who are interested in Navy Air. (Tailhookers are pilots and other crew members who have made an arrested landing.)

Frontier Casino, Las Vegas

Some people went to the Tailhook Convention for the seminars. Some people went for the gambling. Some went for the Las Vegas shows. Some went for the Tailhook banquet. Most of us went for a little of all of these.

This was my first Tailhook convention. The banquet was more or less the highlight of the weekend. Our squadron managed to grab a table with about 12 seats. We were served a great dinner. I remember it well. It was prime rib and baked potato.

The condiments were on the table. A squadron-mate who I will call Charlie (that's not really his name.) and I ended up sitting beside each other. When he was served his meal, he grabbed one of the condiment bowls and started plopping its contents on his potato. Most of us noticed that it wasn't sour cream like Charlie obviously thought.

It was horseradish for our prime rib. Charlie had taken nearly half a bowl for his potato. Now just about everyone at the table was trying to look like they weren't watching Charlie as he cut the potato and put his first bite loaded with horseradish into his mouth. Then we waited. What would he do? Would he try to hide his error? Would he leave the table? What? He slowly picked up his napkin and placed it over his mouth and discreetly (he thought) spit out the "infected" potato. The whole table rocked with laughter. Charlie looked around acting like "What's so funny? I don't get it? Why is everybody laughing?" That caused an even higher level of uncontainable laughter.

Later that night, a visiting Australian admiral was introduced as the keynote speaker. He began his talk with normal opening comments but then it became obvious that he had had too much to drink. He was absolutely wasted. He was weaving back and forth, belching, and slurring his words. I had never heard of Foster Brooks. That's who it was. It was very early in his comedy career. His act was to pretend to give speeches appearing to be drunk. After about five minutes we were standing on our chairs, waving our white cloth napkins around in circles, whooping and laughing. It was the funniest thing I had ever seen.

The first joke that put us onto him was when he was talking about his wives:

"I've been married three times.
All three of my wives died.
The first died from eating poisonous mushrooms. The second also died from eating poisonous mushrooms.
The third died of a fractured skull - (pause) - She wouldn't eat her mushrooms!"

The next day Tailhook '70 was over and we were on our way back to Lemoore, California for more training and preparation for our next cruise.

Wing-fold Take-off

Sometimes pilots get overwhelmed by the fast-paced conditions of a training environment. I have experienced this in the past and have, in my haste, forgotten to complete certain checklists. I know how easy this is to do. I missed a rather important item on a checklist while flying a carrier qualification flight during my training in Beeville, Texas. That oversight could have proven to be fatal. I was lucky.

One dark night during the fall of 1970, an A-7 pilot (not from VA-93), took off at N.A.S. Lemoore and immediately reported having trouble controlling his aircraft. It wasn't turning properly. He said the controls "felt funny." He couldn't see his wings since it was dark, but he said everything looked OK to him as he made a right turn to the downwind leg of the landing pattern. His aircraft was light- loaded, meaning that he didn't have a full "bag" (tank) of fuel. So, he was within weight limits to land which is exactly what he wanted to do.

He was granted priority permission from the tower to land his jet. After landing, observers on the ground noticed that his wings were folded. I never realized that an A-7 could fly with half of each wing vertical, but this one did. Not recommended.

"Toe"

In the summer of 1970, upon return from the *Ranger* Cruise, I teamed up with Bob "Skip" Graff and Tom Hernon to rent a three-bedroom house in Lemoore. Very few pilots enjoy living on board the Naval Air Station in the B.O.Q. (Bachelor Officer's Quarters). It's much more relaxing to live in a regular house away from the base.

Bob had just returned from his cruise in A-4 Skyhawks on *U.S.S. Coral Sea*. His squadron was transitioning to the A-7E. The "Echo" version of the A-7 had much improved electronics and a more powerful engine.

Bob had an accident while in Hong Kong on *Coral Sea* – He was returning from liberty in Hong Kong on the ship's officer launch. The seas were rough and as he was disembarking, his foot was crushed between the recovery barge and the launch. He was taken to the hospital and had to have his right big toe amputated. Fortunately, when he recovered, he was still able to fly and earned the call sign of "Toe."

Unfortunately, one night in March 1971, while on a night practice bombing flight at China Lake, Bob's jet crashed and he was killed. He was a great guy and a really good friend. I was told by someone, trying to console me about Bob's death, that if you stay around naval aviation long enough, you will lose friends. It is a dangerous profession. So true.

N.A.S. Fallon Weapons Detachment

By January 1971, we were more than halfway through our training for the next cruise. One important part of the training was working with the other squadrons in the air wing. The entire air wing flew to Fallon, Nevada to begin this phase of training. The first few days at Fallon, were strictly about bombing at the target ranges that were just south and east of the field at N.A.S. Fallon. Once we were airborne from Fallon, we would do a zig and a zag, and we were at the target. Each pilot had opportunity to fly several bombing missions during the first week to sharpen his bombing skills.

During the second week, we had several coordinated air strikes as an air wing. These were commonly called alpha strikes. The coordinators of our training had also arranged to have some "MIG's" (Air Force aircraft) try to attack our strike group. The idea was that our F-4's should intercept them allowing the strike to proceed to target unscathed. This was all very realistic and was great training.

At the end of the two-week detachment, some of the pilots were given awards for their excellent bombing. Several guys in VA-93 received awards: Commander Rudy Kohn, Lieutenant Tom Laakso and Lieutenant Roger Thompson. The E-2 squadron commander received a special award. The E-2 is a twin-engine turbo-prop aircraft used for early warning and radar. It is not equipped for bombing, but they joined in with the spirit of things one day, by flying over the target at 200 feet and dropping a sack of flour from the airplane. Their award for this effort was a practice bomb (25-pound inert bomb) with a "Gold Medal Flour" decal on it. A great gag. Everybody loved it.

Now we were ready for our next cruise.

E-2 squadron award
Gold Medal Bomb

CHAPTER 6

U.S.S. MIDWAY - FIRST CRUISE

April 1971 – March 1972

Events in the Navy and Worldwide During This Time

February 24, 1972   Vietnam
North Vietnamese negotiators walked out of the Paris Peace Talks to protest U.S. air raids.

July 22, 1971
Commander Rudy Kohn was relieved by Commander Carl Erie as Commanding Officer of VA-93 (aboard *U.S.S. Midway*)

Crossing the Pacific

On April 16, 1971, Air Wing Five embarked on *U.S.S. Midway* for another WESTPAC (Western Pacific) cruise. I had put my car and other belongings in storage and reported aboard. This time I was able to plan a little better and was allowed a foot locker (a 1½' x 2' x 4' lockable metal box) for the personal belongings that I wanted to take with me on the ship. We would be gone for approximately six months.

The trans-Pacific trip would take two weeks, including a stop for a few days' liberty in Hawaii. Prior to pulling into Barbers Point, Hawaii, we had several practice bombing flights, primarily over Kahoolawe, one of the Hawaiian Islands. Kahoolawe was an uninhabited island, used as a naval bombing range. After a few days of flying and liberty in Hawaii, we were on our way again to the Philippines.

Diamond Head

During the transit from Hawaii to WestPac, we expected to be "intercepted" by the Russians. It seemed like a big game that they knew we were coming and would send out one of their long-range bombers to fly over us, just to let us know that they knew we were here. In preparation for the inevitable flyover, we had pilots standing by around the clock in their aircraft, ready to launch with five minutes notice. If an unknown contact was spotted on radar, several aircraft would launch, and another group of pilots would man up to follow them 15 minutes later.

VA-93 Alert Assignments Posted in the Ready Room

The first aircraft off would be a pair of fighters, a photo aircraft, and a tanker (aircraft that carried extra fuel to give to other planes). They would intercept the inbound Russian aircraft and escort him the entire time he was within 50 miles of *Midway*.

The game: They wanted to let us know that they knew we were coming and we wanted to let them know that we knew that they knew.

Another Survival School

When we got to Cubi Point, Philippines, our squadron was sent to J.E.S.T. - Jungle Environmental Survival Training. Our first day of J.E.S.T. was spent in the classroom. The next day was in the field. For our field day, we were divided into small groups to be trained by a Negrito. These indigenous men were very knowledgeable about jungle survival. Some of the older Negritos were World War II vets.

We followed them around all day, watching and trying to learn what we could from them, knowing that if we ever had to eject from our jet over Vietnam, we would most likely be trying to survive in a jungle like this one. They showed us how to make utensils from vines: forks, cups, even plates. They showed us how to get water from what they called "water vines." It didn't taste all that great, but it was a survival liquid.

During our training, one of the pilots in my group tried to get a water vine for himself. He chopped the vine down and cut off both ends just as our Negrito showed us, but when he went to drink by holding the vine up, the Negrito shouted, "No!" The pilot stopped and we all looked around at the Negrito. He said "Not good – no drink." At that point, we realized that survival in the jungle might be a bit more difficult than we thought.

When a pilot ejects from an A-7, he has a parachute attached to his shoulders and a package of survival equipment attached underneath him (in the "seat pan"). We all agreed that if we ever had to eject over the jungle, what we wanted most of all, in our seat pan, would be one of these Negritos.

After this school, we were ready to fly combat missions over Vietnam. The U.S. was not bombing "Up North," so we would be working with F.A.C.s (Forward Air Controllers) in South Vietnam and Laos. On May 18, 1971, we found ourselves positioned on Yankee Station again.

Case Three Approaches

Yankee Station was a busy place in 1971. Sometimes there were as many as three carriers on Yankee Station at the same time. Carriers would generally stay "on the line" for about three weeks, staggering their arrival and departure times so that there was always someone on station.

For our first few days on the line, we would be called the White Carrier (flying during daylight only), then we would switch over to be the Red Carrier (flying noon to midnight), and then for the last week or so, we would be the Black Carrier (flying midnight to noon).

When flying at night or in marginal weather, the ship would operate a Case Three recovery. Every returning aircraft would be given marshal (holding) instructions: a radial, distance from the ship, and altitude that the pilot should use to position his aircraft in a holding pattern, along with a "push- over time" (a time to leave the marshal pattern and begin his approach to land). One aircraft might have "210 at 25 miles and 10,000 feet, approach time 28." The next aircraft would have one mile further and 1,000 feet higher and one minute later: "210 at 26 miles and 11,000 feet, approach time 29." The push-over times were normally one minute apart. It was very important that a pilot began his approach on time, so that the aircraft would be properly spaced for landing.

The initial phase of the approach was a steep descent (4-6000 feet/minute) to 5000 feet, then a shallower descent (2000 feet/minute) to 1200 feet. At ten miles, the pilot would lower landing gear and flaps and slow to 150 knots and eventually to approach speed. For the A-7, this was approximately 125 knots or 145 miles per hour. When he intercepted the glide slope, he would reduce power to establish a rate of descent that would keep him on the 3½ degree glide slope.

At ¾ mile, 300 feet above the water, the pilot was instructed to "call the ball." At that time, he would report seeing the visual glide slope information on the Fresnel lens ("the ball") to the L.S.O., who was monitoring his approach, by saying "301, ball, state 2.5." The L.S.O. would respond, acknowledging that he was watching the aircraft, by saying "Roger Ball." Then the pilot would fly the approach, just like he had been trained.

Wrong Way Approach

Sometimes things didn't go as planned. One day, after all the other aircraft had landed, an aircraft was returning from the beach (from Da Nang). The ship's radar was not working so the pilot was flying an approach without radar monitoring. He was given the ship's heading and was flying on that bearing to break out of the clouds and land. At the end of his approach, he reported being at 2 miles and still in the clouds.

L.S.O.s on the L.S.O. platform

The L.S.O.s were straining their eyes to pick him up visually, but the base of the clouds was 400 feet, and at 2 miles he would be around 800 feet above the water, so they told him to "Keep it coming."

The pilot told the L.S.O.s that he was on bearing at one mile, still unable to see the ship, followed shortly by "Tally-ho," meaning that he saw the ship. Then he said, "Oh no! Waving off!" The pilot went to full power on his engines and flew over the flight deck center line and the wires --- heading the wrong way. The L.S.O.s heard the full power and then looked over their left shoulders towards the roll out end of the flight deck to see this jet climbing back into the clouds, heading toward inbound aircraft.

They got it all straightened out and he was able to land a short while later. It was very fortunate that no one was on approach at that time coming the right direction.

What's Your State?

When a pilot gets his marshal (holding) instructions, he begins calculating how and when to turn in his holding pattern to pass over his appropriate holding fix (position) at the assigned approach time. Sometimes this takes several circles in holding. I remember being in my holding pattern for 20-25 minutes at times. It gets quite boring ... just flying circles in the sky. Sometimes, I would think about the approach and landing that I faced in the pitch-black and would say to myself, "The rest of world is sleeping. What in the world am I doing out here?"

From time to time, while we are holding, Marshal Control (onboard the ship) would call each aircraft to find out how much fuel they had remaining. The fighter aircraft (F-4s and F-8s) were generally of a higher concern, since they burned fuel at a much higher rate than the bomber aircraft. Marshal Control would call us, one by one, "301, say your state." We would answer with our fuel state. "301, state 2.8", meaning that we had 2800 pounds of fuel.

One particularly boring night, Marshal Control was checking fuel states and we all heard this bored F-4 pilot joking. It sounded like this:

Marshal Control:	"Rock River 112, say your state."
Pilot:	"Minnesota."
Marshal Control:	"Say again."
	"Rock River 112 say your state."
Pilot:	"Your state."
Marshal Control:	"Rock River 112, I say again,"
	"Say your fuel state."
Pilot:	"Your fuel state."

Can you imagine the pilot smirking inside his aircraft? Most of the other pilots waiting to land were smiling at this amusing interchange – something to break the monotony of flying around in circles.

Finally, the controller got tired of this game and said. "Rock River 112, say cancelling instruments and proceeding visually." Then we heard, "Rock River 112, state 4.7."

Game over.

Saint Elmo's Fire

One particularly nasty night, I was flying over the South China Sea, returning to the ship for landing. My wingman and I had to pass through some heavy clouds with embedded thunderstorms. We were under radar control and our controller was giving us the best headings to fly to avoid the storms.

As we were traversing the weather, I noticed a greenish glow on the nose of my aircraft. I had never seen anything like that before. I wondered, "Should I be concerned about this glow? It sure is strange." It looked like static electricity and appeared to be crackling, but of course I couldn't hear it. It was outside of my aircraft. It gradually formed into a ball that seemed to be about six inches in diameter.

My jet was flying fine, but there was this strange ball of something on the nose cone. It couldn't be solid. Anything solid would have blown off at the speed we were flying. What was it? Was I in the "Twilight Zone?" Was this something supernatural? No – I found out later that it was Saint Elmo's Fire, a rare condition that occurs in and around thunderstorms, a sort of harmless plasma that looks like static electricity.

The ball started rolling towards me from the nose of my jet. As it got closer and closer, I started pushing myself further and further back in my seat, but there was nowhere to go. The ball magically came through the front windscreen and was less than five feet from my anxious body, which was compressed against the ejection seat as far back as it would go. Then the ball gradually disintegrated and soon was completely gone. I didn't know what it was and was wondering if I should report it to our maintenance guys when I returned to the ship. Was there something wrong with the aircraft?

I mentioned it to another pilot after landing and he just laughed – unconcerned. He told me, "There's nothing wrong with the jet. It's just Saint Elmo's Fire." My wingman had a similar experience that night. I wondered "Who was Saint Elmo?"

Mach One Test Flight

Towards the end of the cruise I was designated a P.M.C.F Pilot. (Post Maintenance Check Flight) When a jet has any major repairs, it had to be tested in flight before being used operationally. An experienced pilot would fly it and check the systems that were repaired to determine if they are working properly in the air and if the jet was safe to fly. If it was, it would be returned to operational status.

On one of my first test flights, I was to test the flight controls at high speed. I was assigned to the Cubi Point beach detachment for a few days when this aircraft arrived. It had been flown from the U.S. to replace another aircraft that had been damaged. It had no bomb racks and wasn't even painted with the squadron colors yet. It was a "slick" clean aircraft.

The checklist essentially said to climb to 45,000 feet and push the nose forward while throttling to full power. Then note what the speed was as you were passing 25,000 feet. Nearly vertical at a 60 degree dive angle, roll the jet for 360 degrees to the right and then 360 degrees to the left and then recover by pulling the throttle back below 70% and gradually pulling back on the stick to bring the nose up to level flight. There were some other checks to do as well. I was to evaluate the feel and effect of the flight controls.

That was the plan. After taking off, the climb to 45,000 feet was uneventful. Arriving at 45,000 feet, I nosed the aircraft over, already at full power. I was fascinated at how quickly the Mach gauge increased. I thought this jet might go supersonic – quite a feat since the A-7 was a subsonic aircraft. The gauge indicated .95 Mach, .96, and then .97. The aircraft developed a slight shimmy as I was headed downward in my 60-degree dive. I thought that was simply because I was nearly supersonic and I might be experiencing some transonic vibrations. I had never flown at supersonic speed before so I was in unfamiliar territory. The shimmy was not too bad and certainly controllable so I pressed on with the test.

Then the Mach gauge said .99 and just touched 1.0. At that instant, the shimmying increased dramatically. Soon the aircraft oscillations became more rapid and more violent, not responding to my smooth inputs from the cockpit. Here I was, in my A-7, diving at 60 degrees, passing 26,000 feet, just barely at Mach one with my wings rapidly rocking about 10 degrees left and right. What do I do? What's wrong? Is this normal as you approach the speed of sound? I said to myself "No. This is not right. Settle down, Marty. You can handle this."

I reduced the throttle to idle and then I thought, "A.F.C.S." I should have thought about that earlier. A.F.C.S. = Automatic Flight Control System – It's like power steering for aircraft. The A.F.C.S. was engaged and all I had to do to disengage it was to push a button on the stick. I pressed it and the oscillations immediately stopped. By now I was nearing 18,000 feet. Time to pull out. That took an effort but at least the aircraft responded to stick inputs without oscillating. Without the power steering assistance from the A.F.C.S., it took some extra muscle to move the stick but it was certainly manageable. Soon I was on my way back to the Cubi Point runway with a jet that still needed fixing.

Thunder Storms

Thunderstorms and poor weather were a regular occurrence while we were on Yankee Station. It seemed like at least one out of four flights involved avoiding bad weather.

One bad weather night I was flying a mission into Laos with Lieutenant Commander Greg Wren. Night missions were generally scheduled with two aircraft flying together rather than four. So, it was just the two of us.

There was a huge line of thunderstorms along the coast line of South Vietnam. Approaching the coastline, we contacted Panama Control (a friendly G.C.I. radar site. G.C.I. = Ground Control Interception). They gave us radar vectors to a less intense region of the line of storms and we managed to get over them without too much difficulty by flying over a saddleback (a region where two storms were connected at the bottom but not at the top. You could fly over the lower connected region without actually going into the clouds, which had the shape of a saddle.) We stayed in the clear and headed west to Laos to continue with our mission working with a F.A.C.

After our mission, heading back to the ship, we had to face the same line of storms again. Only by now, they had intensified significantly. Panama Control told us the tops were reported by a B-52 pilot to be well over 40,000 feet. The controller at Panama said he could vector us a more desirable region so that we could "punch through" with the least amount of difficulty. We could see the storms from miles away. They lit up the sky. It was going to be dicey. We would have to fly through the lightning filled storms, in the clouds, for about five minutes. I was thinking, "I don't like it but we can handle it."

As we approached the heavy weather, we could see the flashes of lightning getting closer and closer, all around us. The sky lit up so well that we could see the shapes of the line of storms, even though in between flashes, it was pitch black. As we were about to enter the clouds, I nudged my jet closer to Greg's, watching his green wing tip light get closer and closer to my cockpit. Soon I was right where I wanted to be. The weather soon affected the air around us. It became quite bumpy. Greg was a good "stick" and a smooth flight leader. A good thing, since I didn't want to lose him in this bumpy darkness.

As the clouds got thicker the lightning became more of a factor. Every time a flash occurred, I could see Greg's entire aircraft for an instant and then it was pitch black again and Greg's jet became invisible in the dark. All I could see was his green wing tip light – nothing else. Then vertigo! I couldn't tell if we were turning or diving or climbing and I wasn't taking my eyes off of Greg's aircraft to check my instruments. Not right now. This cycle of lightning flashes and complete darkness occurred another three or four times before we reached the other side of the line of storms and were in the clear. After that, the sky was clear all the way back to the ship. What an experience!

Case One and Zip Lip

During daylight hours, when the weather was acceptable, the ship would operate a Case One Recovery.

The aircraft in each squadron would be assigned a holding altitude where they would circle in formation with their tailhooks down until the Air Boss announced that the flight deck was ready, by saying "99 Schoolboy, Charlie five."

Switchbox F-4s (VF-151) coming into the break in right echelon

99 meant "everyone," Schoolboy was the call sign for *Midway* and "Charlie five" meant the first aircraft should be landing in five minutes. The Air Boss was a senior Commander who was in charge of and responsible for the flight deck and the safe launch and recovery of the air wing aircraft.

When the "Charlie" was announced, the aircraft at the lowest altitude would circle and descend to a point three miles astern the ship and fly in formation, in right echelon, parallel to the ship down the starboard (right) side of the ship to the break at 800 feet. The aircraft would "peel" off or break at 15 second intervals turning left to parallel the ship in the opposite direction, while slowing down to lower landing gear and flaps and slowing to approach speed and descending to 600 feet. Then directly abeam the landing area, each aircraft would start its left approach turn turning to parallel the ship again lined up on the landing centerline. Then the pilot would fly the approach and land.

When one squadron's aircraft vacated its holding altitude to land, each group of aircraft above would move down a thousand feet to the next lower holding altitude. The aircraft at the lowest altitude would descend and fly into the break as space permitted. All of this was done with minimal talk.

During most Case One recoveries, Midway operated "zip-lip," which meant no radio communication unless there was an emergency. The Fresnel lens being turned on was the signal to Charlie. The air boss would say nothing. Normally there was no need to use the radio during a Case One recovery. The pilot on landing approach would not call the ball, but the L.S.O. would flash the "cut lights" to acknowledge that he was watching. The cut lights were green lights above the ball, easily seen by the pilot.

Midair Collision

Case One recoveries in marginal weather conditions called for extreme caution. If there was significant low cloud cover, the stacked aircraft would have to fly through the "holes" in the cloud cover in formation to get to lower altitudes. When there were aircraft above and below a deck of clouds, there was a high potential for aircraft collision.

On October 19, 1971, Midway experienced one such disaster. We were operating zip-lip under Case One rules with marginal Case One weather. There was a broken cloud layer at 2500 feet. I was a Landing Signal Officer (L.S.O.) in training and was on the L.S.O. platform with several other L.S.O.s and L.S.O.s in training. For some reason an E-2 Hawkeye was orbiting below the cloud cover at about 2000 feet.

E-2 Hawkeye

The E-2 is a large turboprop aircraft with radar saucer on top of the fuselage. Normally, because of the size of an E-2, he would have been at the top of the stack of orbiting aircraft and one of the last to land. But for some reason on this day, there he was below the clouds, holding low.

A flight of three A-7s circling above the clouds flew down through a hole in the clouds at the same time the E-2 happened to fly by underneath the clouds. One of the wingmen from the A-7 flight crashed into the E-2 … wing to wing. The E-2's wing broke off at the wind-fold position. He lost half of his wing. The Air Boss saw the collision and shouted "Mid-air. Mid-air." over the radio. I was watching the aircraft on final approach, but when I heard the Air Boss, I looked up to see the E-2 with one wing intact and the other half gone. He rolled and turned over in the direction of the broken wing and almost immediately crashed nose down and inverted into the Gulf of Tonkin. A rescue helo got to the crash site within seconds, but the aircraft sank immediately. It was gone and all five crew members lost.

The A-7 was still flying but had a major catastrophic hydraulic failure. He was told to head for the beach to an emergency field to land. However, the aircraft didn't make it and the pilot had to eject.

I couldn't believe what my eyes had just seen. Two aircraft and five guys lost in the space of just a few minutes.

Hong Kong

In between each of our line periods (three to four-week time periods spent in a combat zone), *Midway* would transit to a port for approximately a week while the ship replenished. The crew would get some well-deserved time off. Most of the time, we visited Cubi Point, Philippines. Other ports visited were in Japan and Hong Kong. Hong Kong was the highlight of the cruise for me. *Midway* anchored in the harbor about two miles from the Fleet Landing. When liberty was announced, the men and officers were already lined up for the 25-minute trip to the beach. The crew really looked forward to Hong Kong. There was just something mystical about visiting China.

The Hong Kong Hilton was built on the side of a small mountain and had a wonderful view of the harbor. A group of the officers from VA-93 decided to rent a room at the Hilton from which we would base our sight-seeing and trips. We called this room our "Admin." This would be a place where we could meet, socialize, hang out or crash for a night. Since the Admin was not very private, many of us got our own rooms or doubled up so we could have a place with some semblance of peace and privacy. The rooms at the Hilton were rather pricey but I was an unmarried 0-3 (Lieutenant). What did I need money for?

Prior to "hitting the beach," I was told that I should get a suit, professionally made by a Chinese tailor. So, on my first full day in Hong Kong, I went to a well-known tailor shop – Lo Hi Shin's. The tailor took all of the appropriate measurements (I never knew there were so many). I selected the material and style I wanted. And on the last day of our 7 day visit to Hong Kong, I had two perfectly fitted, three-piece suits, tailor made for me and at a very reasonable price.

One of our squadron pilots got married while we were in port. Sonny Kifer (Nathan) and his wife to be, Helen, had made these plans months before. On the appropriate day, the squadron officers took the Star Ferry across the harbor from Hong Kong to Kowloon where after employing several taxis to take us to the church, we joined up with Sonny and Helen for the celebration. Shortly after the wedding, Sonny resigned his commission in the Navy. He didn't finish the cruise with us. Sonny and Helen were happily married, living in Louisiana, where they still live today.

Sonny and Helen Kifer

One of the highlights of any port visit is dining and there were some incredible restaurants in and near Hong Kong. One great restaurant that we visited was Gaddi's in Kowloon. To get to this restaurant from Hong Kong, you had to take the Star Ferry across Victoria Harbor to Kowloon, and then get a taxi for the short ride to Gaddi's Restaurant. The cost to ride the ferry was about two Hong Kong Dollars (less than 50

Star Ferry

cents US). Gaddi's was just about the fanciest restaurant I had ever seen in my life. They specialized in French cuisine.

About twelve officers from VA-93 went on this trip. We were not disappointed. It was worth the effort. I even remember what I had for that dinner - rack of lamb. It was amazing. Rack of lamb is now my favorite meal. The service was outstanding. We had three waiters hovering around the table to see to any needs or wants that we had. – not asking us anything, just watching and waiting to see if we needed anything. I remember dropping a fork that I was using on the floor next to my chair. I reached down to pick it up, but before my hand got there, one of these observant waiters had snatched it up and put a new clean fork next to my plate.

Great food! Great service!

Another quality restaurant was in Aberdeen, which was located on the opposite side of the mountain from Hong Kong. This restaurant was on a boat and served seafood and traditional Chinese food. A Floating Restaurant. There were several ways to get to the restaurant. We took the "over the mountain" route. First, we took a cable car up to the top of the mountain, where the view of the Aberdeen harbor was spectacular. Then we used taxis to go down the mountain to the waterfront

Floating Restaurant in Aberdeen

and then hired a junk (a small boat) to ferry us out to this outstanding, floating restaurant. This was the first time I had ever tasted shark's fin soup. The Chinese food was excellent. Quite an experience, well worth the effort it took to get there.

Wine

Lieutenant Commander Greg Wren reported to VA-93 shortly after we reached the Gulf of Tonkin. He was a very interesting guy with lots of life stories. He told us of the time he met John Wayne and played a game of chess with him (Greg won!). As the famous movie star was leaving, he said, "Well, I enjoyed it." Then, he stuck his head back in the doorway and said, "The hell I did."

One evening after dinner, we went to a Hong Kong lounge (bar), where the band (Chinese musicians) played great, mostly American music: James Taylor, Creedence Clearwater Revival and such. During a musical break, Greg ordered a special bottle of wine that he wanted to share with the eight of us. Greg was a special guy. He was an unmarried Lieutenant Commander. Getting 0-4 pay, flight pay and combat benefits, he had plenty of money and was generous in sharing his money and experiences with others. This bottle of wine cost $175 US. That would probably be equivalent to buying a $700 bottle of wine with today's money.

A waiter brought the bottle of wine to the table. This was no ordinary waiter. You could tell that he was different from the others in the lounge. He wore black pants, white shirt, black bow tie and a black apron. He had a light chain around his neck with several utensils on it. He wore white gloves and had the wine bottle partially covered by a white linen cloth cradled in his hands. Greg told us that he was the sommelier. Then I knew that I was out of my league. I watched Greg with great interest and so did everyone else.

I could tell that Greg was enjoying every moment. The sommelier gave him the bottle which he examined thoroughly, looking at the label and the seal – everything. He nodded and gave the bottle back to the sommelier, who with great flourish screwed the cork screw into the cork, extracted it and gave the cork to Greg. Greg made great show of sniffing it, examining it all around and then nodded again.

The sommelier then poured a small amount of this special wine into a wine glass and handed it to Greg. Greg held it up to the light and examined the wine from different angles. He swirled the wine in the glass and then sniffed it. He said this was savoring the bouquet. Then he took a small amount of the wine into his mouth and swooshed it around. I thought he was going to spit it out, but no. Now he had it in the back of his mouth and was breathing in air over top of the wine. Having no idea what he was doing, I was fascinated with this display. Finally, he actually swallowed the sip.

After all of this, Greg looked up at the sommelier, who was attentively watching Greg's every move. Greg nodded once more and then indicated to the sommelier that each of us was to get a portion of the bottle's contents.

I had never had a glass of anything that cost $175/bottle before, so I wasn't sure how to act. I wanted to appear appreciative but what was I supposed to do? Was I supposed to do all the wine-tasting things before I drank this expensive stuff? Guzzle it down? Sip it? What? What if I didn't like it?

Greg told us that when we got our glass to wait and then at the same time, we should sip it to really taste it. After each of us had been served, Greg proposed a toast, "To the U.S.A. – the greatest nation in the world." We all cheered and tasted this very expensive wine. I sipped it and it was pretty good. Nothing special, though. Certainly not worth putting down $175. But… Thanks for the experience, Greg.

Our stopover in Hong Kong was very eventful and a great break from the rigors of our combat cruise on *Midway*.

Japan

At the end of another of our line periods, *Midway* went to Yokohama, Japan. While we were there, one of the guys in the squadron arranged a dinner at a geisha house nearby. Many Americans have a wrong impression about geishas, thinking that they are prostitutes. Not so. They are trained in skills of serving and entertaining. Every geisha that I ever met was also very charming and engaging.

Ten of us went to the geisha house for a dinner. When we got there, we were asked to remove our shoes and were escorted to a room with a low round table. We were to sit on the floor with our feet crossed or under the table. Five geishas came in, bowed, and were introduced as our waitresses. Two of us per geisha. They sat down between us: guest – geisha – guest, guest – geisha – guest, etc. The geisha was to serve the guest on her left and right. First, they served us some oriental tea, followed by soup, and then the main dish that we ordered. I had sukiyaki. The girls were very attentive and stayed right at the table to assure that we had everything that we needed. If our bowls were empty, they would ask if we wanted more or something else. Yes, they spoke English!

It's impolite in Japan, we learned, to leave food in your bowl. That's a signal that you didn't like it. So, they always asked before giving you more. Of course, they also served us the traditional sake. When the meal was over the geishas performed for us (some Japanese songs and dances.) Then they sang a Japanese version of "Proud Mary," a Credence Clearwater Revival song, which got an enthusiastic round of applause. When they returned to their seating places, they showed us some puzzles and games done with toothpicks, which they seemed to enjoy immensely. All in all, it was a very pleasant, wonderful evening.

The Cubi Catapult

In between line periods, our carrier would most often go to N.A.S. Cubi Point for replenishment and a few days liberty for the crew. Most of the officers would head for the Cubi Point Officer's Club first. The O Club was a nice place and could be used for moderately formal events. It was used by the station personnel as a place to take their spouses and children to dinner and entertainment. That is – until a carrier air wing pulled in. The officers in the air wing were rowdier than most of the station officers would like, so they generally stayed away when a carrier was in port.

Even so, most of the time the officers in the air wing were somewhat restrained in the O Club. However, behind the Club was another building that had a bar and the famous Cubi Catapult. This mini-club was built to withstand abuse. It was made completely of concrete blocks, so unruly pilots could do little damage to the facility. The "windows" were made of chain link fencing. Drinks were all served in plastic glasses.

The main attraction in the mini-club was the catapult. The catapult mechanism had an "aircraft", resembling a 55- gallon drum with a hole cut out for the pilot, mounted on rails. It was equipped with a safety harness, seat belt and a lever that released the tail hook. The aircraft would be propelled by pressurized nitrogen tanks for about 2 feet to a speed of about 15 mph and then released.

After release, the pilot had to estimate precisely when to snap down the hook lever to catch the wire. There was only about a six-inch region (and a fraction of a second) where the hook would catch the wire. Dropping the hook prior to or after this very short region would result in a miss. Pilots who missed the wire continued down the rails to a 30-degree incline into a pool of water, which served to slow the aircraft down and douse the pilot. Successful pilots (and not many were successful) were held in high esteem by other pilots and had their names engraved on the mini-club's "Wall of Fame."

Champagne Bottles

The main O Club was much more sedate. If you didn't want to be subjected to drunken pilots and wet officers who had missed on their attempts to catch a wire on the catapult machine, the main club was the place to be. It seemed most of the men and women in the main club knew they should behave a little better here. -- Most of them, but not all of them.

I was with a group of pilots at a round table in the main club by one of the huge picture windows through which you had a beautiful panoramic view of Subic Bay. We were playing a friendly dice gambling game called Klondike (also called 1-2-3). There were about eight of us at the table, not really paying attention to anything else going on in the club, just minding our own business. One by one, our attention was diverted by a discussion behind our table up four steps to where there was a piano bar.

"No. That wasn't the deal."
"I'm not going to do that."
"Well, I'm not going to unless you do it first."
"Won't we get in trouble?"
"Who cares?"
"What do you mean who cares?"

As we turned around to see what this was all about, we saw two fighter pilots from our air wing standing on the top step next to the piano. Upon further examination, I noticed that each of them was holding the neck of a champagne bottle. When one of the guys raised his bottle up over his head in a throwing motion, I realized they were talking about throwing their bottles through the picture window.

> "Are you going to go through with it?"
> "Yeah, if you are."
> "OK, we'll do it together, on the count of three."
> "Wait! Do we throw on three, or say one – two - three and then throw?"
> "Throw on 3."
> "OK ... 1 .... 2 .... 3 !!!"

They both threw their bottles and completely smashed the huge window. What an explosion of noise! Then chaos ensued! People running everywhere, trying to see what had happened and what was going to happen. In the meantime, our delinquents had disappeared.

The next day, both of these guys were told to report to the Commander of the Air Group, or CAG and to bring their checkbooks. After rebuking them thoroughly, CAG told them that they had to pay $500 for the window ($250 each) and there might be some additional punishment forthcoming.

As they left CAG's office, one of them shrugged his shoulders and said, "What more can they do to us? They've already sent us to Vietnam." They obediently wrote their checks and gave them to the CAG's assistant. The assistant looked at their checks and noticed that they had each written a check for $500 instead of $250. He told them "You misunderstood. You paid too much. CAG said the total bill was $500, not a $500 each." One of the pilots waved his hand and said, "Keep it. ... for the next time." They obviously had not learned their lesson.

On October 10, 1971, the cruise was over and we headed back to the good ole USA, full of memories of good times, regrets for the bad ones, and sorrow about the guys we left behind.

VA-93 Officers on the USS Midway flight deck.

CHAPTER 7

U.S.S. MIDWAY
THE LONG CRUISE

April 1972 – March 1973

Events in the Navy and worldwide during this time

May 10, 1972   Vietnam
Operation Linebacker began large-scale bombing operations against North Vietnam

June 17, 1972   Watergate scandal
White House operatives were arrested for burglarizing the offices of the Democratic National Committee.

July 13, 1972   Change of Command
Commander Carl "Dad" Erie was relieved by Commander Jerry "Possum" Terrell as Commanding Officer of VA-93 (onboard *USS Midway*)

July 1972   Vietnam
Jane Fonda toured North Vietnam.

January 22, 1973   Roe v. Wade

The U.S. Supreme Court overturned state bans on abortion.

January 29, 1973   Change of Command

Commander Jerry "Possum" Terrell was relieved by Commander Doug Clarke as Commanding Officer of VA-93 (onboard *USS Midway*)

February 11, 1973   Vietnam

The first American prisoners of war were released from Vietnam.

Early Departure

Midway and Carrier Air Wing Five were scheduled for their pre-cruise Operational Readiness Inspection (O.R.I.) on April 6th, 1972. We all knew that the peace negotiations in Paris were not going well and we would likely be headed for another combat cruise in the West Pacific in May.

On that day in April, I was leading a flight of four A-7s from N.A.S. (Naval Air Station) Lemoore. We were heading for *Midway* to land and begin the inevitable drills and exercises that go with an O.R.I. As we passed over Los Angeles, we cancelled our instrument plan with Los Angeles Center and transitioned to visual flying. This meant that we would be responsible for maintaining a safe distance from all other aircraft while navigating to our objective without assistance from the controllers on the ground. *Midway* was supposed to be stationed just west of San Clemente Island, which was south-southwest of Los Angeles. So, we initially headed in that direction.

Each A-7 has navigational electronics which indicated the direction to various navigational beacons located on the ground and on ships. When I switched my navigation electronics to give the direction to *Midway*, it indicated northwest. I thought my equipment was broken (it should have told me to go southwest), so I asked the other guys in the flight to tell me what heading they were getting. Everyone was indicating northwest. We figured that must be where she was. Maybe this was part of the O.R.I. We turned to the northwest and contacted Schoolboy Marshall who told us to contact Schoolboy Tower. "Schoolboy" was the call sign for *Midway* and Schoolboy Tower was the Air Boss's frequency.

The Air Boss told us to "Buster" and "Charlie on Arrival." Buster meant to hurry – waste no time. Charlie on Arrival meant we would be landing as soon as we got to the ship – no holding – no delay. Then we got a clue as to what was going on. He told us that Schoolboy was making 50 knots of wind over the deck. She was going somewhere in a hurry. We all wondered why. When we saw *Midway*, we noted that she was heading north at high speed – perhaps her max possible speed. The wake was enormous.

Landing with such a high wind was unusual for us and involved great care with our power during landing approach. The L.S.O.s (Landing Signal Officers) reminded us of this as we entered the landing pattern. Being well briefed and well trained, there were no difficulties in landing our jets. After securing our planes, we headed for the ready room. When we got there, we found out that the O.R.I. had been cancelled and we were heading back to N.A.S. Alameda in Oakland, California. We would dock later that evening (Thursday) and would be leaving for our WestPac (Western Pacific) Cruise on Monday - seven weeks early. We had three days to store our belongings and take care of any personal business. We knew that things were getting hot in Vietnam and this time, when we got there, we were heading up north! (Flying over North Vietnam was significantly more dangerous than flying over South Vietnam)

On Monday April 10, we left San Francisco, passed under the Golden Gate Bridge and headed west. Some of the wives from the air wing and ship's company had driven to

Midway on the way to WESTPAC approaching the Golden Gate Bridge

the Golden Gate Bridge and were standing on the bridge, holding an American flag as *Midway* passed under.

I was a bit teary eyed watching this, knowing that there was tremendous support for us and that these loyal women were also making a monumental sacrifice. Their husbands would be gone for seven months or longer.

After a short stop in Hawaii, we were on our way, once again to the Gulf of Tonkin and Vietnam

While we were transiting the Pacific, President Nixon ordered the renewal of bombing of Hanoi and Haiphong. *Coral Sea* and *Hancock*

Midway wives on the Golden Gate Bridge holding an American flag

were already on Yankee Station. They were joined later in the month by *Kitty Hawk* and *Constellation*.

On 16 April 1972, aircraft from *Coral Sea, Kitty Hawk* and *Constellation* flew missions in the Haiphong area in support of U.S. Air Force B-52 strikes on the Haiphong petroleum products storage area in an operation known as Freedom Porch.

The bombing of the North had begun. *Midway* arrived in the Gulf of Tonkin for her first combat missions on April 30. We were stationed at Dixie Station, which was south of Yankee Station. Our first few days would be spent working with Air Force F.A.C.s (Forward Air Controllers) in South Vietnam. After we got our feet wet,

Diamond Head looking from Midway as we head out to sea.

we would move north and begin our missions in North Vietnam.

Being on combat duty on April 30 qualified us for a whole month (April) of combat pay, as well as free postage on any letters that we sent. I was a smoker in those days and was amazed when I found out that the price for a package of cigarettes was only 20 cents...not the usual 75 cents a pack. You could buy a carton of cigarettes for $2. No tax was charged.

Vietnam was a scary place, but the names of the cities and provinces were almost musical. Names like: Haiphong, Hanoi, Kep, Dong Hoi, Da Nang, Saigon, Pleiku, Hue, Quang Tri, Ha Tinh, Chu Lai, Ninh Binh, Hong Gai, Thanh Hoa, and Vinh.

A-7 – tanker
Approaching the catapult.

Then there were locations such as: The Mekong River, The Hourglass, Mu Ghia Pass, Ban Karai Pass, Ho Chi Min Trail, Happy Valley, and Tan Son Nhut Air Base.

Mugs

There were two main groups of men on Midway...ship's company and the air wing. The ship's company took care of the myriad of day to day responsibilities that needed to be handled to keep the ship safely running and feed and care for the 5000 men on the ship. An air wing consisted of eight to ten squadrons (the men and aircraft). Ship's company and the air wing each had approximately 2500 men.

One aspect of being in an air wing on a combat cruise is that you get to meet some very interesting people. Lieutenant Commander "Mugs" McKeown was one of those interesting people. He was the operations officer for VF-161 (Fighter Squadron One Six One).

During our transit of the Pacific, we had several opportunities to fly training flights as we anticipated the combat experiences that lie ahead. Most of the pilots were very tense (especially the pilots who had not flown combat missions) and were nervous about flying up North, but not all showed it. Mugs was the kind of guy that would relieve that tension. Prior to one of our transit flights, I

F-4 Phantom from VF-161

was in my aircraft going over some pre- taxi checks when an F-4 taxing toward the catapult caught my attention. I looked up and saw the pilot was wearing a gorilla mask over his helmet.

It looked like this big monkey was taxiing the Phantom. It was Mugs. I remember laughing out loud. It was a real tension-breaker. We talked about it for days. Some of the guys mentioned that they couldn't wait to get to Hong Kong, so they could get some kind of mask to go "one-up" on Mugs. That would never happen. Mugs was always one step ahead.

As I mentioned previously, in the 1970's the Russians would send a long-range bomber, usually a Bear, to intercept U.S. carriers when they were transiting the Pacific, just to let us know that they knew we were there.

We were going to be ready for them. During the Pacific Ocean transit, "Alert five" pilots were in their aircraft sitting on the catapults, around the clock waiting for the inevitable flyover. Eventually, an inbound Bear was scanned on radar. So, *Midway* launched the alert five aircraft (all launched within five minutes of the alert announcement.) 2 F-4 Phantoms, 1 F-8 Crusader Photo jet and one A-6 tanker.

The F-4s "bustered" to intercept the inbound Russian aircraft. Sure enough it was a Russian Bear. As fate would have it, Mugs was the pilot of one of the F-4s. He joined up in formation on the wing of the Bear and flew right next to him for the Bear's entire flyby of *Midway*. The F-8 photo plane was recording the entire flight in pictures. There were quite a few great shots. Looking closely at some of the photographs, you could plainly see one of the Phantoms was being flown by a gorilla. It had to be Mugs. What a hilarious photograph: An American F-4 being piloted by a gorilla flying in formation with a Russian Bear, and if you looked more closely at the Bear, you could see three heads looking through the one small window in the back of the plane, one had a camera. You could only imagine what those Russians were thinking. "Have the Americans run out of pilots and started training monkeys to fly?" When the Bear left the area and our aircraft landed, some of these pictures were posted around the ship to the delight of all the crew.

This happened in late April, before we got to the Gulf of Tonkin. Just about one month later, in May 1972, Mugs had another adventure.

On May 23rd, while leading a section of F-4s on a Combat Air Patrol North of Hanoi near the enemy airbase at Kep, Mugs and his R.I.O. (back seat - Radar Intercept Officer), LT. Jack Ensch, along with their wingman engaged six North Vietnamese MIG aircraft in what has been described as one of the longest and most exciting dogfights of the war. When it was over, Mugs had shot down two North Vietnamese MIG-17s. Mugs and Jack Ensch were subsequently awarded Navy Crosses.

When they returned to *Midway*, they came into the break at 800 feet as usual, but nearly supersonic (not usual). The Air Boss announced that the incoming F-4 crew had shot down a MIG and was going to fly by the ship on a high-speed pass. As they passed the ship, Mugs pulled his F-4 straight up doing the traditional Victory Roll. While the aircraft was pointed straight upward, the pilot rolled his aircraft for 2-3 complete rotations. Everyone on the flight deck enjoyed a moment of celebration.

S.A.M.s

In addition to the air to air threat from the Vietnamese MIGs, we also faced the ground to air threat from A.A.A. (triple A or Anti- Aircraft Artillery) and S.A.M.s (Surface to Air Missiles). S.A.M.s were guided from the ground by a radar controller. Sometimes, A.A.A. used radar as well,

VA-93 Ready Room One

making the rounds much more accurate. In the cockpit, a pilot would have several indications that radar was operating and tracking his aircraft.

There was a visual display in the cockpit with a strobe pointing in the direction to the radar site, and many sounds transmitted by electronics into the pilot's headset: High frequency chirping meant that the enemy radar was scanning. Higher frequency chirping meant that the radar was tracking your aircraft. Low intensity warble meant that the S.A.M. radar guidance was operating. A more rapid warble meant the radar was actually sending guidance commands to the missile.

Upon hearing the warbles, a pilot should be searching for the S.A.M. and readying himself to maneuver his aircraft and avoid the missile when it got close. These warbles sounded like "doodle – loodle – loodle – loodle …"

A Fiasco

My first up close and personal experience in a high threat S.A.M. environment came during an Alpha Strike to a region near the Vietnamese city of Than Hoa. It was one of *Midway's* first strikes in the North and my first major Alpha Strike. These strikes involved the coordinated efforts of the pilots and crew of over forty aircraft, all attacking targets in the same general area at the same time. The CAG (Commander of the Air Group) briefed and was to lead the strike flying an A-6 Intruder. However, his aircraft had some major mechanical issues and couldn't be flown. These mechanical safety issues, commonly called "gripes" were often found by pilots while on deck, shortly after start-up. Other "gripes" would be noticed in the air and reported when the aircraft returned. Some of these were more serious than others and needed to be repaired before the aircraft could be safely flown again. Other less urgent gripes would be fixed as time permitted. Since CAG's A-6 was broken, leading this strike of over forty aircraft fell to a junior officer, CAG's wingman. It was this junior officer's first flight as a strike leader.

As the flight of over forty aircraft went "feet dry" (crossed over the coastline), we were all in our strike formation, looking for our targets, but none of us could find the targets we were assigned because the lead aircraft had navigated incorrectly and brought the entire strike group to the wrong target area. The junior pilot in the lead A-6 rolled in on this unknown, unseen target and everyone else followed him. As I rolled in, following my leader and looking for the target I had been assigned, I heard "Doodle – loodle – loodle." and saw something that looked like a telephone pole zooming by my A-7 about 300 feet to my right. I was in a 45-degree angle dive accelerating to 450 knots, looking for my target when with my peripheral vision, I saw the missile go zooming by. If it were tracking me, there would have been nothing I could have done to avoid it. The S.A.M. proceeded harmlessly through the strike group, causing no damage to any air wing aircraft. I never saw it explode and assumed it never did or that it exploded above us. When I reached 5000 feet of altitude, I noticed my leader dropping his bombs, so I followed him and dropped mine. Unfortunately, I had no idea where they went, since we dropped our bombs in the jungle without sighting our target. Later we found out that our real target was several miles away from where we dropped our weapons. On the way back to the ship, after this mission, I thought to myself, "This was complete and utter chaos."

Haiphong

Shortly after that chaotic flight, I was assigned to a strike on Haiphong. Our division of four A-7s was assigned to bomb a power plant in the city. At least this time, I saw the target before I had to roll in on it. As we approached Haiphong, we heard the normal electronic sounds indicating S.A.M.s in the area but I couldn't locate them. I was looking frantically for a missile because if one was tracking me, I wanted to be able to evade it. I was flying on the wing of my leader, depending on him to maneuver us as necessary. Just as I was about to roll in, I saw two orange smoke clouds at my altitude about 200 feet to my left. S.A.M.s. They had been tracking and exploded near us, but fortunately didn't hit or damage us. I never saw them! I made a decision at that time to be even more "eyes out" during strikes. If a S.A.M. was tracking me, I wanted to see it.

Sneak Attack

After these two incidents, I flew many more strikes and soon got the hang of looking out for and avoiding S.A.M.s. Then on one flight, I got still another lesson. The strike group had just bombed a target near Than Hoa and my division was exiting, heading back to *Midway*. I relaxed since we had just gone "feet wet" (crossed the enemy coast heading outbound). We had been feet wet for about a minute when I noticed a S.A.M. explode on my left about 500 feet from our group of A-7s. Where did that come from? The first indication I had that there was a S.A.M. in the area was the explosion. I hadn't been scanning very intensely since there were no S.A.M. indications in my headset and we were heading away from the target area. I had relaxed and let my guard down.

After landing, during my debrief I learned that sometimes the Vietnamese would fire a S.A.M. without radar guidance, guiding it manually somehow, hoping to catch an aircraft off guard. He surely caught me off guard! I was very fortunate to learn that lesson without losing my aircraft or worse.

Pagodas, S.A.M.s and Jane Fonda

One of the most frustrating aspects of this "war" was all of the rules that the pilots had to follow, primarily about where not to fly and where not to bomb. It made sense that we weren't to fly or bomb in Cambodia, since Cambodia was more or less a neutral nation. Of course, the enemy knew that as well and used Cambodia as a refuge.

However, when the no-fly rules were extended to the enemy nation, they became questionable. There were numerous pagodas and religious buildings in Vietnam. We weren't to fly or bomb within three miles of them. Do you want to guess where the enemy put its Surface to Air Missile (S.A.M.) sites?

In July 1972, a famous American actress, Jane Fonda visited North Vietnam, supposedly in support of American P.O.W.s. The Vietnamese used her visit to further their own cause. In the end, she did more harm than good, since she ended up, in our eyes, being unsupportive of the American government. While she was there, another no-fly, no-bomb zone followed her around. We were not to be where she was.

Night Reconnaissance

One of the most common missions that we flew over North Vietnam was called a "road recce" (pronounced "reck – ee" which is short for reconnaissance). A road recce is basically a search and destroy mission. A flight of two aircraft would be given a region to cover … to explore, searching for targets and destroying the most lucrative ones that were found.

At night, the lead aircraft would carry parachute flares to illuminate any area that seemed to have targets. He would fly at 5,000 to 8,000 feet of altitude with all of his external lights off, with the exception of a dim tail light. He would be virtually invisible from the ground. Unfortunately, he was very hard to see from the air as well.

That was the trail aircraft's responsibility. He was to fly above and behind the leader at or above 9,000 feet. Each aircraft had an instrument that told the pilots how far apart the lead and trail were. So, with that information, the lead searched for targets in the dark and the trail jet followed, obviously keeping the lead's dim tail light in sight. Of course, they communicated with U.H.F. radio as well. If the lead aircraft changed his general direction, he would radio the trail aircraft so that he would realize the dim tail light that he was tracking would be heading in a different direction.

If the lead found something, he would circle back and position himself above the target at a lower altitude and deploy one parachute flare. If possible, the lead would deploy his parachute flare without circling back. The flare would fall for a short distance and ignite, hanging from a parachute. At that point, the lead would turn and climb so that the trail jet could roll in on the target, if he could see it. If he couldn't, he would wait until the lead positioned himself and rolled in on it. Then the trail aircraft would follow in turn. When rolling in, the attacking jet would "go black" (turn off all exterior lights) and then after the bombing run when the jet was safely climbing and at a safe altitude, he would go "lights on" again, so that the other jet in the pattern could see and avoid him.

One night, I was the trail aircraft. As we were scouting a medium threat area near Vinh, my lead told me he was about to release a flare. I saw the flash as the flare was ejected from the pod that the lead was carrying. People on the ground must have seen it too, since three A.A.A. (Anti-Aircraft Artillery) sites immediately opened fire. I could see three sets of tracers converging on the spot where lead had just popped out his flare. These gunners were good. When I saw the tracers, I remembered that every tenth round was a tracer round. It seemed like they had fired about sixty tracers at the lead aircraft. Wow, that was 600 rounds coming up at the lead aircraft. This was a busier area than we had originally thought.

Even though I was not targeted with this barrage, I was very distracted by the tracers as well as the flare that had just ignited below where lead was flying. The guns kept firing even though they couldn't see us. Perhaps they were firing at the sounds of our engines.

In all of the commotion, I lost sight of the lead and had no idea where he was or where the target was. Eventually, I looked at my instruments to find that my lead was 3.8 miles away from me. Too far. No wonder I couldn't see his dim tail light. He had not turned to circle over the target. He told me he thought his aircraft might have been hit and continued straight ahead.

He said that his instruments indicated that he was OK. Unfortunately, it took a while for us to get visual contact again. By that time, the flare had extinguished, and the target on the ground had plenty of time to hide and was most likely completely out of sight. So, we decided to leave that area and were able to complete our mission at another spot.

Alpha Strikes

We flew many different kinds of combat flights in Vietnam: Alpha Strikes, Recce (reconnaissance), Search and Destroy, Surface

Surveillance, Photo Reconnaissance, Ground Support (with Forward Air Controllers), and others.

Alpha Strikes were used to send a maximum number of aircraft (and therefore maximum ordnance) on a set of closely grouped targets in a high threat area. This group of aircraft would launch, join up and then proceed to the target.

Normally the strike group would have 32 bomber aircraft in two groups of 16, one group in front and the other behind and above the first group.

There would be two or more sections of two Iron Hand aircraft. Iron Hand aircraft had a special mission. They would

A-7 Corsair II
Iron Hand - Landing on Midway
Picture by permission of Doug Howe

each carry four AGM-45 Shrike air to ground missiles and were tasked with protecting the bomber aircraft from S.A.M.s. Shrikes were radar tracking missiles. If a radar site illuminated (sent out radar signals), the shrike could home in on the beam and track it to destroy the radar. If the radar site shut down after the Shrike was fired and had been tracking, the shrike would still make an attempt to hit the site, by maintaining its current track.

Similarly, several sections of two fighters would position themselves over threat airfields to ward off any MIGs. Also, there were:

tanker aircraft -	with fuel for the fighters and any other aircraft that needed it,
radar aircraft -	to track friendly and enemy aircraft, and
electronic warfare aircraft -	to send electronic signals that were intended to confuse enemy radar operators so that they couldn't lock on the strike aircraft effectively.

After join up, the main strike (bomber) group would proceed to the target while everyone else did the mission they were assigned in support of the bombers, all coordinated.

Armstrong

A-7 aircraft were bombers, not fighters. When an A-7 would see an enemy MIG aircraft, the pilot would hope that the MIG was being chased by F-4s. Nonetheless, A-7 pilots liked to have air-to-air missiles (Sidewinders) on board when they were flying in a MIG threat area. My personal strategy was that if I was head to head with a MIG, I would fire my Sidewinder at him right away and then go full power, push over and run, hoping to deter his attack. If I ended up in a one on one combat scenario with a MIG, I would most likely lose since the MIG could easily out maneuver an A-7. My hope was to put as much distance as possible between my aircraft and the MIG, while calling in the fighters.

The air wing armed all A-7s with one AIM-9 Sidewinder, which provided some small measure of comfort to the A-7 pilots who were hoping they would never have to use it.

One afternoon, I was assigned to the second group of an Alpha Strike heading for a high threat area in North Vietnam. CAG was leading the first group. There were several commands given to the group as we headed toward the "beach." One of them was "Armstrong." When that command was given by the flight leader, all aircraft were to ready their bombs, by selecting switches in the cockpit, so that the only thing a pilot had to do was press the "pickle" switch and the bombs would be released. The pickle was a button located on the control stick and the pilot almost always had his right hand on the stick. The most important switch that was turned on at that time was the Master Armament Switch, which must be on in order to fire or drop anything.

As this Alpha Strike was nearing the beach, CAG announced, "99 Schoolboy, Armstrong." All 32 aircraft began arming their weapons, but then "whoosh …" A missile flew from the second group up to and through the first group. Planes were jerking up and left and right as the missile went by. CAG yelled "What the $*&* is going on? Who fired that missile?"

One of the A-7s had an electrical malfunction and when the pilot turned on his Master Armament Switch, his Sidewinder fired. He never pulled the trigger. It launched on its own. Fortunately, no one was hurt. The missile hadn't had time to arm, and therefore never exploded. Obviously, CAG was upset. As a result of this malfunction, A-7s weren't armed with Sidewinders during the remainder of the cruise.

The Three Mile Limit

I had always wanted my name in the paper (for some good thing I had done). Who wouldn't want that? *Midway* had a tabloid that was published regularly. I don't remember how often. After one mission, I was actually interviewed and my comments showed up on the front page. Not a big deal, but my name was in the paper.

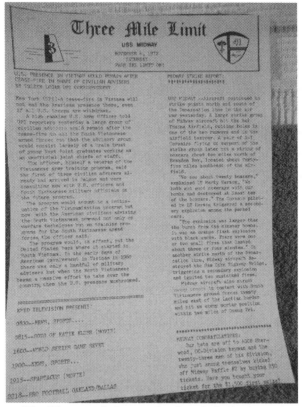

The Three Mile Limit- Midway's "newspaper"

Pre-Emptive Shrikes

Toward the end of the summer of 1972, it seemed that the North Vietnamese had an abundance of S.A.M.s because they were firing more and more of them at our aircraft. The air wing staff came up with a brilliant idea to reduce the number S.A.M.s being fired at our Alpha Strike bombers. Pre-emptive Shrike firings.

Normally, the Iron Hand aircraft wouldn't fire their missiles until they had a positive indication of radar tracking. Then the pilot would turn his jet toward the site, pull up the aircraft's nose (about 15 degrees nose up), and fire. All of that took time. Often, by the time the Shrike was launched the radar site would have already fired its S.A.M. and would be nearly finished tracking. So, they would shut down and our missile had nothing to track. The trick was to have the Shrike missiles locked on immediately after the sites powered up so that they could track and explode before the S.A.M. guidance was complete. When that happened, the radar site would be destroyed and no more missiles could be fired from that location until repairs were made or the radar was replaced.

Our new strategy was to have the Iron Hand Aircraft on each side of the strike group as it headed in. At a projected time, the Iron Hand aircraft would each fire two missiles toward the known locations of S.A.M. sites. The missiles (eight of them) would be in the air and coming down as the strike aircraft were approaching their roll in point. When the S.A.M. sites powered up to attack the bombers, the Shrikes would acquire a lock on the radar and "WHAM!" Scratch one radar site and the bombers would have a good day with very few S.A.M.s. The first two days we tried that strategy, some S.A.M.s were fired at the bombers. The third day … no S.A.M.s at all.

We kept that strategy going for several weeks, when we received a message from the brass in Saigon. The message essentially said: "No more pre-emptive Shrike firings. These missiles cost $25,000 each and the enemy obviously has no more S.A.M.s or they would be firing them." My thoughts: "Are you kidding me? What are they thinking? A missile cost $25,000! How much did an A-7 cost? What was a pilot worth?"

Under the new guidelines, we were allowed to fire our Shrikes only if we had a positive radar lock on, but not pre- emptively. Obediently, we stopped the pre-emptive firings the next day. We were told that we could pre-emptively fire unguided (much cheaper) decoy missiles instead. These missiles would not track anything. The brass told us, the radar operators would see them and shut down, thinking that they were Shrikes. The Vietnamese were not dumb. It only took one day before they figured that strategy out. Then, the sky was filled with S.A.M.s again.

We had lost no aircraft while using the pre-emptive firing strategy. Now it appeared that we would very likely lose some while using this new ineffective strategy. So, since we were allowed to fire Shrike when we had a radar lock on the enemy radar, the unofficial Iron Hand philosophy became, "Fire one missile pre-emptively each with any kind of radar tracking indication. Be ready to fire others as needed." The number of S.A.M. firings reduced significantly after that and all was well. Very few Alpha Strike losses from S.A.M.s from that point on.

F-4 Phantoms

F-4 Phantoms were fighter aircraft. They had a mission that was vital to the safety of the air wing and the whole aircraft carrier. They were to keep enemy aircraft away from any and all friendlies. To that end, they had two main mission assignments: TARCAP and BARCAP

> TARCAP – Target Combat Air Patrol. This mission was to keep MIGs from attacking the strike bombers while they were on the way to and from their target. Normally the Phantoms would station themselves over enemy airfields if no MIGs were airborne. If MIGs launched they would engage and attack them.

> BARCAP- Barrier Combat Air Patrol. This mission was the same except it included keeping MIGs away from the carrier strike force as well. During this mission, the Phantoms would generally be stationed over the northern Gulf of Tonkin, between Haiphong and Yankee Station.

> CAP missions were launched every time the ship was conducting flight operations in the enemy territory. Most of the time, it was just "boring holes in the sky." No action, just boredom. But once in a while, MIGs would launch and the Phantoms would go to work.

The rest of the time the F-4s were used as bombers. The F-4 was not designed to be a bomber, just as the A-7 was not designed for air to air combat. Each aircraft was built to serve a different purpose. The Phantom pilots wanted to fly bombing missions because there were only a limited number of CAP missions. They wouldn't be "boring holes in the sky." Bombing missions were always exciting.

One problem with the Phantoms was that they always seemed to need fuel. They used afterburners to launch and almost immediately after take-off they were calling "Tanker posit," which is a transmission to the tanker pilot asking him for his position, so that they could join up with him and add some gas to their tanks.

My MIG "encounter"

Don't get me wrong, Phantom pilots are great guys and love what they do. I love what they do, too. They did such a great job that I only saw one airborne MIG the entire time I was flying over North Vietnam. They really knew what they are doing.

The one time I saw a MIG, I was heading back to the coast after an Alpha Strike in North Vietnam. I was the lead aircraft for a section of two A-7s. We were powered up trying to exit the area as quickly as possible, when I noticed a flash at my one o'clock position, about 3-4000 feet above me and five miles out. As I watched, I soon could tell it was a MIG19. The MIG passed by into my three and then four o'clock and eventually was pretty far behind me. I just about broke my neck twisting around to see if he was going to turn into me and try to get a shot at us. Soon, I lost sight of him. Then I noticed another flash at my two o'clock at the same altitude the MIG was at. There they were -- a pair of Phantoms, in hot pursuit of the MIG. I breathed a sigh of relief. Still looking around for MIGs, I passed the coast and headed safely back to Schoolboy.

F-8 Crusaders
Sights and Sounds

The F-8 Crusader was a very cool aircraft with several different missions. The Crusaders on *Midway* were "photo- birds." Their mission was to take B.D.A. (Bomb Damage Assessment) photos immediately after alpha strikes as well as other photo reconnaissance. Other air wings had Crusaders with a fighter mission, similar to the Phantoms.

Aside from its distinctive airframe, the Crusader had several other unique characteristics. Unlike the Phantom's adjustable afterburner, the Crusader had an all-on or all-off afterburner. When burner was selected by the pilot on the catapult, just before launch, it sounded like an explosion. "Boom!" Also, when the Crusader took off or landed, the pilot "raised the wing" giving the F-8 better landing characteristics.

F-8 Crusader
on landing approach with wing up

The characteristics of the Crusader's ejection seat required the pilot to wear leg restraints (The pilots called them garters.) These were straps the pilot wore above and below the knee. The restraints had metal loops in them through which a line was fed and attached to the floor of the jet. This line would protect the pilot's feet and legs by pulling them together during the ejection sequence, so they wouldn't flail around or hit the sides of the cockpit as the seat and pilot were propelled up the rails.

F-8s in combat

The F-8 was also named "the Last of the Gunfighters" because the fighter version of the Crusader had air to air cannons as well as missiles. The following story was related to me. One day, a section of two F-8s (from another aircraft carrier) was patrolling north of Hanoi when they were "jumped" by four MIG-19s. The MIGs were almost immediately behind the Crusaders. The pilots turned hard into the MIGs and the fight ensued. At one point during the engagement the F-8s got separated. When the lead F-8 reacquired his wingman, there was a MIG behind the wingman.

The lead transmitted excitedly, on the radio: "Snake two. There's a MIG on your tail! There's a MIG on your tail!" The lead was busy himself and he lost contact with his wingman again. Then as quickly as it happened the MIGs "bugged out" (left the area). The lead tried to find the wingman again for mutual support. He called, "Snake two, what's your position?" The answer came back, "I don't know where I am but I'm going a thousand miles an hour!"

F-8 Emergency Landing at Cubi Point

Occasionally aircraft were flown back to Cubi Point for maintenance and upkeep. Pilots that flew them from the ship to Cubi were often responsible to test the aircraft when the maintenance was complete. I was on one of these test flights in my A-7 when I heard this exchange between one of *Midway*'s F-8's (also on a test flight) and the Cubi Point tower.

F-8 Crusader Picture by permission of Peter Batcheller

605:	"Cubi Tower, this is 605. I need priority handling for my landing."
Tower:	"Roger 605. Are you declaring an emergency?"
605:	(after a short pause) "Affirmative"
Tower:	"What's the nature of your emergency?"

When a pilot declared an emergency, ground crews were scrambled just in case the aircraft crashed or the pilot needed assistance when he landed. Many people were put in motion. There were medical response teams, fire trucks, and ordnance crews … all positioning themselves to assist the pilot if needed.

I was the only jet in the landing pattern. I was doing practice landings (called "touch and goes"), but I decided to land to give 605 all the room he needed.

605:	"It's a personal emergency. My aircraft is fine."
Tower:	"605, Are you hurt? Will you need assistance after landing?"
605:	"Negative. I just need to land as quickly as possible."

Now I knew what the problem was. The pilot of 605 needed to get to a bathroom and it sounded like he needed to go … badly. I landed my jet and taxied back to the flight line when I noticed 605 entering the pattern making a very tight close turn for his landing. He really was in a hurry.

After I parked my jet, I saw 605 taxiing back to the line. He was taxiing faster than he should have been, but I knew why. I saw him frantically unstrapping as he was taxiing, so he could jump out quickly as soon as the Crusader was stopped and shut down. He parked right next to my A-7. As soon as his F-8 was shut down, he stood up on the seat of his jet. He was grimacing, really in extremis. I was hoping that he could make it. (I had been in that predicament before.) Unfortunately for him, he hadn't disconnected his leg restraints. They were still attached to the floor of his aircraft. As he tried to climb out of his plane, the leg restraints tightened. He tried to put his left leg over to the aircraft ladder but ended up falling over the cockpit rim with his legs attached securely to the aircraft. There he was: legs still in the aircraft and the rest of his body hanging upside down over the edge of the cockpit, kind of like he was on a trapeze, with nowhere to go – no way to move.

That was it. He gave up. It was a valiant effort but, in the end, he smiled a weak smile and relieved himself, while he was hanging there.

Crossing the Equator

The Navy has many wonderful traditions. One of them that we celebrated on *Midway* as we headed for our liberty in Singapore was the equator crossing ceremony: "The Order of Neptune." This Navy tradition is over 400 years old and is "celebrated" whenever a Navy ship

King Neptune

crosses the equator with crew aboard that have never crossed the equator on a Navy ship before. These crew members are called "pollywogs," while the veterans are called "shellbacks."

After a "slimy pollywog" crosses the equator, he is initiated and becomes a "trusty shellback." Normally, the day before the ship actually crosses the equator, there is a special ceremony where King Neptune (a senior shellback) announces the upcoming events to the crew of pollywogs. On *Midway*, we were to have a beauty pageant to entertain the shellbacks, followed (the next morning) by the "royal bath" where the pollywogs had to make their way on hands and knees through piles of trash and garbage (on tarps on the flight deck), while being hosed (with fire hoses) by the shellbacks. We were to eventually make our way to the "Royal Baby" and kiss his belly. The Royal Baby was generally the biggest, fattest guy (a shellback) they could find onboard. When you kissed his greasy belly (greased with lard, oil, slime. You can just imagine), the "Baby"

Beauty Pageant

would grab your head and pull it into his fat and the slime, so you got it all over your face and in your hair. After that, you would proceed to the King and kneel before him as he declared that you were now a trusty shellback. All in good fun.

Singapore and Bob Hope

Late in December 1972, after the Shellback initiation, *Midway* headed for Singapore for eight days R&R. I was assigned to the Shore Patrol for the first two days in port. As a part of my Shore Patrol experience, I thought I would try to get an idea of where to go and where not to go while on liberty. I asked the regular shore patrol sailors to take me with them on their rounds of the city. Unfortunately, we generally traveled the less savory areas so I was not able to find the "good spots."

One night, they took me to Bugis Street. This was a "red light district." There were women everywhere, most of them very beautiful. They were flirting with tourists and sailors trying to get them to pay to have their photographs taken together, inviting them to a bar for a drink, or to their rooms for sex. I commented to the sailors with me on patrol that these women were amazingly pretty. They smiled and chuckled at my comment and one of them replied. "They're not women." Oh my. They were all men ... trans-gender women. This was definitely one of those places to avoid.

After my two days of Shore Patrol was over, Bob Hope and his entourage came aboard *Midway* to entertain the crew with his Christmas Show. The show included: "The American Beauties (dancers), Lola Falana, Roman Gabriel (a professional football player) and Redd Foxx (a well-known comedian). A great show!

Bob Hope

Grande Island

Midway had nine line periods (combat periods spent on Yankee Station) during the 1972/73 cruise. In between line periods, we went to a liberty port for a break for 6-10 days. Singapore was great. We also visited Hong Kong, another great place with lots to do. However, most of our liberty was in the Philippines, since Cubi Point was so close to Yankee Station.

Sparky Pierson, Marty Herzog and Scott "Hoover" Clark at Grande Island

A group of us visited Grande Island while we were in Cubi Point for one of our liberty periods. Grande was located in the Subic Bay, which is where Cubi Point is and where *Midway* tied up while in port there. A short boat ride from Cubi and we were at Grande, well away from Olongapo. We had a bungalow that housed six of us. In the evening, guards patrolled the area, keeping us safe from raiding HUKs (a remnant of guerrillas opposed to Americans from World War II). While we were there, Doug Howe, one the VA-93 pilots composed the catchy song "S.A.M. City" about our flights over North Vietnam.

```
                        SAM CITY
Words by Blue Blazer    To the tune of SURF CITY   As sung by
LTJG Doug Howe          by Jan and Dean            "The RoutePac Six"

Ten SAMS on every run . . .
You know the brief is always boring and the AI's confused now:
SAM City, here we come.
The planes are never ready but you go just the same, now:
SAM City, here we come.
You know you don't need a BN or an RIO, 'cause the Corsair'll
    get you where you gotta go . . .

CHORUS
You know we're goin' SAM City, where it's six to one:
You know we're goin' SAM City, gonna make one run:
You know we're goin' SAM City, not a lot of fun.
You know we're goin' SAM City, it's your Alpha one, now -
    Ten SAMs on every run . . .

You knew you're always nice and cool because you sweat to the bone
    now.
SAM City , here we come.
You know it's off the cat and airborne, leave the hassle behind, now.
SAM City, here we come.
You know we're overhead and rendezvoused, we're all set to go -
With the Phantoms yelling, "Tanker, posit, where did you go?"

Chorus
```

Two of the verses to "S.A.M. City" by Doug Howe

Losses

There were a large number of casualties during this cruise. I can't list them all here, but here are a few that stood out.

Commander Charlie Barnett

He was our Executive Officer. On May 23, 1972, he was on an alpha strike with Lieutenant (Junior Grade) Bill "Hawgy" Monroe. They had bombed their target and were heading back to the coast. XO Barnett gave the flight lead responsibilities over to Bill and took his position behind Bill as wingman. Shortly thereafter, when Bill attempted communication with XO, there was no reply. He had disappeared. We assumed that he had been shot down by either a MIG, a S.A.M., or A.A.A. (Anti-Aircraft Artillery). We never found out for sure.

Commander Barnett's remains were returned to his family in the U.S. for his funeral at Arlington Cemetery, nearly seventeen years later on March 27, 1989.

Lieutenant Mike Penn

On August 6, 1972, Lieutenant Mike Penn was shot down by enemy fire. Lieutenant Commander Greg Wren and I were called in as RES.C.A.P. (Rescue Combat Air Patrol). Greg circled low to try to spot Mike while I covered him several thousand feet higher watching for ground fire at Greg's aircraft. We were hoping to be able to contact Mike and call in the "Big Mothers" (rescue helos) to get him out of there and bring him home.

Even though we were in a high threat area, there was very minimal fire at us from the ground, so we were able to remain on station for 30 minutes or so. Greg could not spot Mike on the ground and we never heard anything from his emergency radio. We found out later that he was captured and became a P.O.W. Mike was eventually released and returned to the U.S. in 1973.

Lieutenant Commander Don Gerstell

One mission that attack aircraft had during the summer and fall of 1972 was "Surface Surveillance." Communist ships were bringing in supplies to southern ports near Vinh along the Vietnamese coast. They would anchor off the coast and under cover of darkness, would move supplies inland on a barge or other craft. Our mission was to be on the lookout for these barges and call in two or four plane air strikes if any were spotted.

On September 7, 1972, while on one of these missions, Don flew into a thunder cloud and was never seen again. We assumed his aircraft was struck by lightning or he was hit by an enemy missile.

On an earlier flight, Don taught me a very valuable lesson. I was leading a section back to the ship. We were feet wet (over the water) in what I thought was a relatively safe region when Don "thumped" me. I was showing about 300 knots in my airplane, when Don went under my A-7 from behind at about 400-450 knots and pulled his aircraft up right in front of me. Less than a second later, I flew right through his jet-wash producing a rather violent "thump" to my aircraft.

I hadn't seen him coming and was completely surprised. If he had been an enemy MIG, I would have ended up in a parachute (if I was lucky). The lesson was pretty obvious. You are not safe just because you are over the water. Never let your guard down.

Lieutenant (junior grade) Mike Bixel (and 4 others)

On October 24, 1972, Lieutenant Bruce Kallsen (pilot) and Lieutenant (junior grade) Mike Bixel (bombardier/navigator) were returning to *Midway* after a night radar bombing mission in their A-6 Intruder. It was a pitch-black night with no visible horizon. They had two hung Mark 82 bombs. (500 pound bombs that did not drop off their aircraft when they bombed their target.) These bombs

A-6 Intruder

could not be jettisoned either. The plan was to bring them back aboard the ship. The extra weight did not take the A-6 over weight limits. So, it seemed to be OK.

When they landed, the right main mount broke off and the stub caught one of the arresting wires and turned the aircraft to the right. This took the Intruder directly down the flight deck towards where the aircraft that had just landed were parked. There were many aircraft and people directly in the path of the A-6. The A-6 was headed for these aircraft and when a crash seemed inevitable, Mike Bixel ejected and was eventually lost at sea. His body was never found. Bruce Kallsen chose to stay with the Intruder. The aircraft continued, slamming into the pack of aircraft before coming to a halt. Several aircraft were on fire, but the crash truck was right behind them and had the fires out in less than two minutes.

This was a major accident. The pilot, Bruce Kallsen survived but five men were killed, including Bixel, thirty or more were hurt, some very seriously. Many aircraft had major damage. At least one went over the side. In spite of all of this, *Midway* flew its missions the next day.

Overhead

While all of this was happening, I was overhead, waiting for my turn to land. I received radio instructions to "Bingo to Danang." (proceed to Danang and land there). Having no idea that there was a catastrophe below me, I obediently headed off to Danang. The controller eventually did say that there was a crash on the flight deck but gave us no indication of how much damage there was or when we were to return.

Landing at Danang at night would be tricky for several reasons.

1) We had carrier pressure in our tires. Tires were inflated to a higher pressure when landing on the carrier. That made the jet able to withstand the impact of the landing. This higher pressure was not the best for landing on a field. If the pilot didn't

apply his brakes very judiciously, the tires could easily blow out and the aircraft could possibly skid off the runway.

2) It was night and we were not familiar with Danang.
   There could be towers and wires between them and other obstacles that we were not aware of. Also, there were mountains around Danang.

3) There were enemy forces nearby. People could be shooting at us while we were on approach.

The landings of all the bingo-ed aircraft went uneventfully. We reported to flight control after securing our aircraft, where we were told to report back the next morning at 1130. We should report to officers' quarters, get a room and then we were on our own. It was about 11 PM. so, after checking in, we went off to the Red Horse Bar, the local Air Force hangout.

We still had no idea of what had happened at the ship. We had a few beers and asked the Zoomies (Air Force pilots) how life was in Danang. They told us they hadn't been rocketed for two nights. So, we were due for an attack. Great! I had my .38 revolver and some flares with which I could fire back. A lot of good that would do.

After getting that exciting update from the Zoomies, I headed off to bed. The officers' quarters were not very elaborate. My room had two sets of metal bunk beds, a closet and a chest of drawers. Oh well, it was only for one night, I hoped. I jumped in the top bunk of one of the beds and set my alarm for 0800, hoping that I would be able to find a place to have breakfast in the morning.

Later that night, I was awoken by a siren sounding some kind of alarm, followed almost immediately by a number of explosions, one of which sounded like it was right in my room. It was outside, but it shook the walls and knocked me off my bunk. This was the attack the Zoomies were predicting. They had told me if there was an attack I should try to get to a bunker, but I felt like that would be a bad idea. I wasn't going outside during a rocket attack. No, thank you. Since I was already on the floor, I crawled under the lower bunk and decided to wait for the "all clear." Soon the attack was over and rationalizing that there wouldn't be another, I went back to sleep.

The next morning, I went outside to see what the damage might be. I noticed a crater, about 2 feet deep, 15 feet from my bunkroom window. That was too close for me. Some of the other pilots said that they fired their pistols toward where they thought the rockets were coming from and were going to ask for a "Combat Action" ribbon. -- Really? Are you kidding me? Not me. I was under the bed.

After breakfast, we reported to the flight line and were soon on our way back to *Midway* for the day's missions.

Close Calls

1) On November 10, 1972, VA-93 pilot Lieutenant Mike Cobb's A-7 was shot down by A.A.A. He ejected successfully and was recovered.

2) Another VA-93 pilot, Lieutenant Bill Beith, was hit by enemy fire as well. Fortunately, he was not shot down, but his flaps were damaged and he couldn't use them. Flaps were needed to land the A-7 on the carrier, because without them the aircraft approach speed would be too high. However, this day, there was more wind than usual and the ship was able to use its speed to generate some excess wind over the flight deck – enough so that an A-7 could be landed safely without flaps. Bill made the approach and safely landed.

3) One night after a search and destroy mission, I was flying back to the ship with my wingman. We had seen quite a bit of A.A.A. in our area that night so we were relieved to be heading "back-ship." After each flight, pilots generally looked each other's aircraft over for battle damage. On this flight neither of us saw any damage to the other, so we proceeded to *Midway* for landing.

After landing, I taxied forward and parked my aircraft. One of the maintenance chiefs climbed up to talk to me. That was unusual. They normally waited for the pilot to climb down to talk to them. He said, "Lieutenant Herzog, are you all right?" "Yes," I replied "Why?" The chief said "Be sure to look at your left wing before you leave the flight deck."

After climbing down, I looked at my left wing. There was a hole about 4 inches in diameter through my flap. The flaps are hollow so nothing inside of the aircraft was damaged. However, about 10-12 inches forward from where the hole was – were two main hydraulic lines, used for flight controls. If they had been hit, I would have lost control of the jet and would have had to eject. That was close.

C.N.O.

During our cruise on *Midway*, Admiral Elmo Zumwalt was C.N.O. (Chief of Naval Operations). The C.N.O. is the most senior officer in the Navy. Admiral Zumwalt was pretty popular with younger officers and enlisted. He had made a series of moves intended to reduce racism and sexism throughout the Navy. These policies were disseminated throughout the Navy using communications called Z-grams.

Other Z- grams authorized longer sideburns, beards and longer hair. Several of the officers in VA-93 decided to grow the longer hair and beards. It didn't take long for us to realize that maybe, for pilots, a beard wasn't a good idea.

There was supposed to be a water-tight seal between your oxygen mask and your face. Having a beard made this seal virtually impossible. I had a

CDR. Erie and LT. Marty Herzog Note - the facial hair.

goatee for a while, but shaved it off when I realized it jeopardized my safety.

In late October 1972, Admiral Zumwalt visited *Midway*. We thought he was going to tell us that we had done a good job and we were going home. As of October, we had been away from home for over six months. The projection was that we would be home by Christmas. That would have made our cruise eight months long. That's long enough to be away from home.

The officers were assembled in the wardroom (where the officers have their meals) to be addressed by the Admiral. After a few introductory remarks, he came to the part of his speech in which I was most interested. I don't remember exactly what he said but it was something like, "Everyone who thinks you will be home by Christmas, raise your hand. …

Not so fast." That was supposed to be a joke, but personally I didn't think it was very funny. Certainly, there was a better way to break the bad news to us. Then he told us we would be extended at least until February.

The Magic Carpet

Our last day on the line was actually February 8, 1973. Then *Midway* headed for Cubi Point one last time to refuel and get ready for the transit home.

During the Trans-Pac home (transit across the Pacific), there was nothing to do, since the cruise was over. When the ship got close enough to the United States, VA-93 pilots would fly our aircraft to Naval Air Station, Lemoore, getting home one day earlier than the rest of the crew. That was a good deal for 10 pilots. Normally a few of the aircraft would be un-flyable. So only the good jets would be sent to the beach. The others would be craned off at Alameda, California, to be fixed and eventually flown back to Lemoore.

There was an even better deal for some of the pilots. There were about 15 pilots in the squadron. Only 10 were needed to fly the aircraft.

That left five. These five plus a number of non-pilots in each squadron took the "Magic Carpet" home. The Magic Carpet was a commercial jet that was chartered to take us from Japan to California. We would get home nearly 10 days before everyone else. Each squadron would select its personnel for this really good deal. I was one of the lucky ones.

After the ship arrived at Cubi Point, about 80 officers and enlisted men were flown by helicopter to Clark Air Force Base (about 50 miles north of Cubi) and flown from there to Tokyo. We were really excited to be going home. On February 11, we all got on the Magic Carpet airplane, found our seats and were on our way. Next stop – U.S.A. One thing I noticed after about an hour on the airplane, was that my pants didn't fit. I hadn't worn my Service Dress Blues for over a year. The "good living" and good food in the Orient went right to my waistline. I knew that when I got home, I would have to pick up my exercise program as well as having some alterations done to my uniforms.

Once we were airborne, they served the Magic Carpet group free drinks. This could have been a mistake! Alcohol and Navy pilots can be a dangerous combination. This situation brought to mind a story about another Magic Carpet flight that occurred a few years prior.

On that particular flight, a good number of the pilots were completely "sauced." They decided to play a trick on the commercial airline pilots that were taking them home. One of the guys said, "Hey, everyone, let's all move to the back of the airplane," knowing that the airline pilot would notice the change in the handling characteristics of his plane if they did that. The center of gravity of the airplane would cause the nose of the airplane to pitch upward.

So, they all moved and stood as far back as they could. Then this comedian said, "OK, now let's move forward as quickly as we can." This would cause the opposite effect. There was no thought of the possible danger of having the aircraft's CG (Center of Gravity) move back and forth and the pilot having to change his trim settings trying to keep up with the shifting. They had actually felt the nose moving up and down when they moved. I guess they really thought this was really funny because they did this back and forth movement for another cycle. Then the captain opened the door to the cockpit and stuck his head out. He looked at the group and they looked at him, and after a moment of silence, the pranksters all burst out laughing. Not the captain, he didn't think it was very funny. The captain went back to the cockpit and made an announcement that they should all return to their seats or he would have to return to Japan. He had the trump card. They all obediently returned to their seats and behaved themselves for the remainder of the trip. There was no more booze served. They were cut off. That memorable flight had a smooth trip the rest of the way.

No such shenanigans for us. We behaved ourselves, looking forward to having the remaining hours of our trip pass by as quickly as possible. Roughly eight hours later, our captain made announcement that we were 200 miles from the California coast. Almost home. When we crossed the coast, all of us let out a big hoot. After nearly eleven months, we were back home again. Home sweet home.

VA-93 Pilots

CHAPTER 8

TRAINING SQUADRON 26
(VT-26)

April 1973 – October 1975

Events in the Navy and Worldwide During This Time

October 10, 1973
Spiro T. Agnew resigned as Vice President of the United States.

April 15, 1974
Patty Hearst was photographed robbing a bank in San Francisco.

August 8, 1974   Watergate Scandal
U.S. President Richard Nixon announced his resignation

August 9, 1974
Vice President Gerald Ford succeeded Richard Nixon as the 38th President of the United States.

April 20, 1975
    The Vietnam War ended with the Fall of Saigon

April 29, 1975
    Operation Frequent Wind was carried out by U.S. 7th Fleet forces

August 20, 1975   Viking program
    NASA launched the Viking 1 planetary probe toward Mars.

Beeville

After a few more months flying A-7s in Lemoore, California, I checked out of VA-93 (Attack Squadron Nine Three), packed my Fiat and headed east – to Texas. I had orders to report to Training Squadron Two Six (VT-26) in Beeville, Texas for duty as a flight instructor. The last time I was in Beeville, I was a student naval aviator (in 1969). So much had happened since then. Now I was a combat experienced pilot who was expected to pass along his experience to new bright-eyed inexperienced students. I would be teaching these students to fly the T-2C Buckeye – their first jet.

When I drove into Beeville, I was low on gas, so I stopped at the first filling station I could find. This was Texas, so I thought "The gas should be cheap here." It was. Gas cost 23.9 cents a gallon. I could fill up for under five dollars! Compare that with the cost of gas today. Today, five dollars won't buy enough gas to move the gas gauge needle.

I had vivid memories of my experiences at Chase Field as a student, but I had forgotten what the town of Beeville looked like. After filling up my Fiat, I drove toward the center of town and came to the only traffic light in Beeville. I thought, "One traffic light in the whole town? There is going to be no 'action' here. This is going to be a long tour of duty."

I was used to living close to big cities while I was in California. Los

Angeles and San Francisco were only a few hours away from Lemoore. What would there be to compare with that, here in Texas? Would there be anything to do? Corpus Christi was the nearest city of any size, but it didn't hold the attraction for me that Los Angeles and San Francisco did. But, in spite of the gloomy prospects for the next two to three years, I decided face reality and look for a house. I didn't want to live on-base.

The housing market was down in those days. So, without too much trouble, I was able to purchase a good new house (my first house ever) in a nice neighborhood. Three of my new neighbors were also instructor pilots in VT-26. Two of them were marine Captains and the third was a navy Lieutenant named Rick Ludwig, who some years later became the commanding officer of elite squadron TOPGUN.

House #1 - 802 South Canyon $23,500

Did you see that price? A new house for under $25,000! Imagine that.

Off-duty Activities

There was more to do in Texas than I had originally thought. "Corpus" wasn't too far away and there were a lot of bars, clubs, movie theaters and other activities there. There was also a great restaurant called the "Red Barn Steak House," about halfway to Corpus. Going to the Red Barn for a steak was well worth the 30-mile drive.

I had a fenced in back yard and decided to get a dog, a pure-bred Irish setter, whom I named Barney. I really enjoyed him. Barney was a lot of fun, but he wasn't too bright. He had an inbred desire to chase birds and other small animals. I thought that was pretty normal in a dog, but with Barney it was more obsessive than other dogs I had seen. One day, I was driving home with him. I made the mistake of leaving the passenger side window about halfway down. He was sitting in the passenger seat (no seat belt, obviously). He saw another dog outside and instantly jumped out of the window. I was driving about 35 miles per hour and he jumped out of the car! As I said … not too bright. He landed safely and was on the run after the other dog. I had to stop and turn around to go back and get him. When I got to where he had jumped out, I saw him and the other dog going around in circles sniffing each other's behinds. He was a very friendly dog.

Barney was so much fun, that I decided to get another Irish setter as a companion for him. I named her Samantha, or just Sammie. Before long we had a whole family of 12 setters. Mama, Papa and 10 little ones. Since they were pure bred, I was able to sell the eight of them that survived puppy-hood. I was considering going into the breeding business but realized that the market for Irish setters in the little town of Beeville would be rather small.

Guns in Texas

Just about every truck that you saw in Beeville had a gun rack in the back window. I didn't have a truck, but I wondered why everyone seemed to want to have a gun prominently on display in their vehicle. As it turned out, hunting was very popular in Texas and there was almost always something to hunt year-round. So, I purchased a 12-gauge shotgun and joined the festivities. A 12-gauge was perfect for bird hunting and there were a lot of birds in the area, primarily ducks. During hunting season, a group of us went duck hunting several times each month and almost always came back with a good number of these water fowl. Great feasts generally followed each of these hunting trips.

I also purchased a 7-millimeter rifle. I'm not sure why. Maybe it was my way of trying to be cool. A 7-millimeter rifle was powerful enough to bring down an elephant. There weren't any wild elephants in Texas, but there were deer. One Saturday, I decided to take my rifle to a local quarry to "sight it in." My rifle had a 4X scope (with cross hairs) that you could use to aim at your target, but the scope had to be pointing where the rifle bullet was going to go. So "sighting it in" required taking a few shots at a target followed by adjustments to the scope. A shot and then an adjustment, another shot followed with a more precise adjustment, until the scope and the rifle were aligned.

When I set out to do these adjustments, my inexperience with firearms of this size became apparent. I set the rifle on a mound of dirt with my target (a 2-foot by 2-foot piece of cardboard) about 100 yards away. I sighted in through my scope and fired. When I fired, the rifle recoiled so I couldn't see where the bullet went. I was hoping to see the puff of dirt where the bullet landed. Not seeing that puff, I went down to my cardboard target to see where the hole in the cardboard was. Sadly, there was no hole. I was way off. My shot completely missed the cardboard target. I would have to fire again, but how would I know where the bullet went this time? As I prepared for my second shot, I thought that maybe I jerked the rifle as I fired the first round and that was why it didn't hit the cardboard. This time, for some reason, known only to the gods of stupidity, I thought if I don't hold the rifle, it won't jerk. That was certainly true, so without holding the rifle, I sighted through the scope once again and fired. Dumb! I hadn't given any thought to the fact that even though the rifle didn't jerk, it still recoiled, and the recoil was powerful. The rifle slammed right into my face. Ouch! That was it for sighting my scope. I was off to the hospital. I had a big headache and was bleeding profusely right over my right eye. What was I thinking? Eyes are very valuable to pilots and I nearly lost one of mine. I still have a scar over my right eye as a memento of this occasion. After this event, I wondered if I would have to courage to ever fire this rifle again. I did fire it again, although it was several years later.

Music

My old doctor friend, George, from Pensacola training command days had resigned from the Navy, but we kept in touch. He stayed in the reserves and managed to get assigned to Beeville for his annual two weeks of active duty. He brought his drums. During the middle weekend of his two weeks, I threw a party at my house and we provided the music. I found an enlisted guy, Rodney, who played the bass, so we had a three-piece band. It was really great seeing George again.

Shortly after George left Beeville, I found another musician, Kenny, also enlisted, who played the drums. So, we had a band with Rodney on bass, Kenny on drums and me on guitar. We played several gigs during the next few months and practiced once a week in my living room. We set up our equipment right next to the rack of stereo equipment I had set up in my living room and jammed away. My neighbors didn't seem to mind since our practices didn't go too late and we weren't practicing an exceptionally high decibel level. We named the band "Two Plus One" because two of us were enlisted, one an officer and two of us were white, one was black. We thought that was an appropriate name. I realized some time later that hanging around these two enlisted guys was not too bright and contrary to navy policies.

When I returned from Christmas leave that year, I found that my house had been broken into and I was robbed. Nearly all of my expensive stereo equipment was taken. I had purchased most of this equipment in Sasebo, Japan, during my last Midway cruise. Interestingly, my guitars and amps were not touched. They were in a back room of my house, so I thought that maybe the robber didn't see them or know they were there. I later found out that Kenny was the burglar, but I had no way of proving it and I couldn't find him. Two weeks later, Kenny was found dead in a park in the city. I didn't know it at the time (I found out weeks later), but Kenny was involved in drug trafficking and was killed by the drug distributors with whom he was working. I didn't even know he was using. He sure did fool me. I never recovered my stereo equipment.

Air to Air Gunnery

I was assigned to VT-26 as an instructor pilot. One of the most demanding phases at this level of training was air to air gunnery. I remember how hard it was for me when I was a student. Surely as an instructor, it would be easy. Not so. It was still hard. It was very challenging to hit all the checkpoints in the gunnery pattern right-on, and most students, seeing the pattern for the first time were completely overwhelmed.

Each time a gunnery group went on a flight, the pilot towing the banner would take off first and head to the target area, which was over the Gulf of Mexico. Then, the remaining jets would take off, rendezvous and fly out to the range to locate the tow pilot and set up the pattern. If there were no ships below us, the pilots (including students) who were qualified, would be given permission to fire live rounds on the banner.

When the tow pilot returned the banner to the field after the flight, it was examined for hits. Each pilot's rounds were painted a different color, so we could know how many hits each of us scored. The holes in the banner would have a circle of paint around them revealing whose bullet it was. Of course, competition was keen.

There were ten flights in this phase of training. For the first flight, the instructor flew the jet from the front seat with the student in the back, observing, taking it all in. If the weather was OK, the instructor would actually fire the guns at the banner (being towed by the safety pilot.) The next three flights were duals (the student in the front seat with the instructor in the back), and then a fifth flight, the check flight, where the student was evaluated and determined "safe for solo." After that, the real excitement began. The student had five flights as a solo and was allowed to fire his guns on the last three (if the tow pilot, who was the range safety pilot, granted him permission).

The student solo flights were especially challenging since there was no one in the back seat to give the student constant feedback. The safety pilot had to diligently watch each solo student in the pattern, especially if he was a "shooter." Completing this phase of training gave student pilots a tremendous feeling of accomplishment, especially if they were able to score hits on the banner.

Muffled Communication

One beautiful crystal-clear afternoon, I was flying in the gunnery pattern with Ensign Paul Smith who was flying his first gunnery flight from the front seat. He needed a lot of help, but most students did. There were two radio transmissions the student was to make in the pattern. If for example, he was number two in the pattern, he was to call "Two's in" and "Two's off," at certain places in the pattern. Simple transmissions! Paul was flying an acceptable pattern for his first time on the controls, but then after a while, he started shaking his head from time to time and his transmissions were garbled.

Instead of "Two's in," and "Two's off," it was "Fthoos thinn" and then "Fwwthoos aaff." The way my student communicated was a direct reflection on my instructional abilities. There were several other instructors in the gun pattern and they were listening. I told Paul to speak more clearly. He nodded his head, but the garbling and head shaking continued. Eventually, running out of patience, I told Paul, "I've got the airplane." He put his hands up in the air as a signal that he was relinquishing control of the jet. While I flew the jet around the pattern from the back seat, making the correct voice transmissions, he took his oxygen mask off and shook it downward, as if there was something in it. Ahhhh! It became clear why he was having a hard time. He had thrown up in his mask. No wonder he couldn't be understood. That must have been awful! When he put his mask back on after cleaning it out, things were much better. We finished the flight without further incident.

Carrier Qualification

Another challenging phase of jet training was carrier qualification. Upon completion of this training, the student could call himself a "Tail Hooker," (a pilot who had landed on an aircraft carrier). The training consisted of ten flights in the landing pattern at Beeville or Goliad (an outlying field) and one flight "at the ship."

VT-26 had three L.S.O.'s (Landing Safety Officers) assigned. (I was one of them.) It was our job to train groups of student pilots, to prepare them for their first carrier landings, usually on *U.S.S. Lexington*. Approximately, once each month, each L.S.O. would be assigned a class of 6-12 students. For each of their field landing flights, the students would launch and enter the landing pattern under the control of the L.S.O. It was our job to instruct these students, refining their landing skills as future carrier pilots.

The L.S.O. would position himself on the "L.S.O. Pad" adjacent to the runway where the planes would land. Each of the student pilots would take off and enter the landing pattern, observed by the L.S.O. The landing pattern was oval shaped with six to eight jets, evenly spaced, about 30 seconds apart, meaning there would be one jet on approach every 30 seconds.

The student would "call the ball," indicating he saw the ball on the landing mirror – "601, ball, three point five." Three point five was an indication of how much fuel he had remaining in his aircraft. The L.S.O. would acknowledge him by saying, "Roger ball," and following up with any helpful advisory information such as, "You're high," "Steady with the nose," "check your lineup," or "watch your power." Students needed a lot of verbal help in the pattern. Once they got to the fleet, they would need only minimal help.

As the jet got closer to landing, the advisory calls became commands, such as "Power!" which meant add power now, or "right for line up" – slight turn to the right to correct a drift, "Attitude" which meant to carefully raise the nose of the jet, or "Wave Off!" which meant to apply full power and climb. Students were given wave offs routinely on every flight to make sure they responded safely. After each normal landing, a student pilot would immediately add full power and take off and follow the jet ahead of him in the pattern, turning left 180 degrees when he had the proper spacing.

After eight to ten landings, the students would be told "Full Stop" by the L.S.O., which meant that when the pilot touched down on this pass, he was to retard the power, brake the jet and return to "the line" (the parking area) and shut down the jet. The L.S.O.s would soon join the students for debrief, to discuss their strengths and weaknesses.

Each landing approach (also called a pass) was graded by the L.S.O. The grades correspond to a one, two, three or a four. In L.S.O. lingo:

> a grade of four is called "OK," (the best grade)
> a grade of three is called "Fair,"
> a grade of two is called "No Grade,"
> a grade of one is called a "Cut" (dangerous approach).

After their ten flights "at the field," they generally had a social get-together as a class and made an optional bet with their instructor L.S.O. Normally, the stakes were a beverage of the student's choosing. It could be a bottle of some liquor, a case of beer, or soda … whatever he chose. To win the bet, the student had to perform well at the ship. There were two ways to do that.

There are four arresting wires on *Lexington*. The target wire is the number three wire. If a pilot is right on glide path with correct airspeed and line-up, he should "catch" the number three wire. To qualify at the carrier, a student had to make four safe arrested landings. If he caught the three wire on three of his four landings, he would win the bet. Another way for the student to win the bet would be for him to have three OK passes at the boat. That was very rare.

So, if a student caught three number three wires or had three OK passes, he won. Otherwise the L.S.O. won. Since very few students won the bet with their L.S.O., I had a very well stocked liquor cabinet by the end of my tour with VT-26.

Flaming Hookers

After their carrier qualification flight, the students who qualified had a party, generally at the home of one of the L.S.O.'s. Each student would be invited to celebrate with their instructor by drinking a "Flaming Hooker." A Flaming Hooker is Drambuie served in a small liqueur glass. The surface of the Drambuie is set on fire just prior to consumption. Two of the students would be "fire marshals," each having a large glass of water, in case the "Flaming Hooker drinker" spilled any of the burning liqueur on himself. If that happened, he would immediately be doused by the "student fire department." Students that had moustaches often had their facial hair singed during this ceremony and were quite often clean-shaven the next day.

Charlton Heston

Each month when the time came for the students to land on the carrier, the squadron L.S.O.'s would fly out to *Lexington* before the students arrived, so we could be in position when they came. After we landed aboard *Lexington*, we would normally go directly to Air Operations to find out when our students were scheduled to arrive at the ship. We wanted to be ready for them, so they heard a familiar voice when they rolled out on approach for their first carrier landing.

On one of my trips to *Lexington*, I noticed a new captain in the Air Operations room. When this new captain turned around, I noticed he wasn't a real captain at all. He was an actor … Charlton Heston. I always thought he was taller. He was wearing a navy uniform with captain's insignia. I found out that a movie was being filmed on *Lexington* and Charlton Heston was the main actor. The movie was *Midway*.

I thought all movie stars were snobs, but Mister Heston proved me wrong. When he noticed us, he came over to our group, shook our hands and asked us what our jobs were on the ship. He seemed genuinely interested and visibly impressed when we briefly explained our assignments as flight instructors and L.S.O.'s. As he was leaving, he commented, "That sounds like exciting work. Good luck. Great to meet you."

More Cars and a Motorcycle

Car #7 – 1973 Volkswagen Kombi - A few months after arriving in Beeville, I realized that I wanted to travel around Texas on my weekends off. A camper sounded like a great idea. New campers were very expensive, so I decided to buy a van, and have it converted into a camper. In July 1973, I purchased a Volkswagen Kombi for $3500 and took a week's leave to drive it to Chicago to have it converted into a pop-up camper. I used this camper to travel to many of the "interesting places" in Texas such as San Antonio, Houston, the "Rattlesnake Round-up" in Uvalde and Big Bend National Park.

Car #8 – 1975 Dodge Mobile Traveler - I enjoyed camping so much, that I eventually decided to get a larger camper. Since the cost for new campers was so high, I opted for a used one. In May 1975, I traded my Kombi in for a very slightly used, almost new, 1975 Dodge Mobile Traveler. This was a much bigger vehicle, with a queen- sized bed, a kitchen, bathroom, a heater and hot and cold running water (battery

1975 Dodge Mobile Traveler

powered). All the comforts of home. I still had my trusty Fiat Spider, but the Mobile Traveler was my companion on most of my weekend trips.

Motorcycle – I bought another vehicle while I was in Texas. A Honda 350 Motorcycle. Shades of "Easy Rider." I could hear the music as I visualized myself cruising down the road with Dennis Hopper and Peter Fonda. It was cool having a motorcycle in Texas. I drove it to work most of the time. Finding a parking space was always a snap.

Snow in Texas

It rarely got very cold in Beeville, but when it did you could tell that the Beevillians were not accustomed to it. One day at work, we noticed that it was snowing outside. No one in the squadron could recall ever seeing snow in Beeville. It wasn't a blizzard or anything like that, just a half inch or so, maybe not even that much, but it was snow and was laying on the grass and on the roads. I was a little anxious about driving my motorcycle home on the slippery roads.

I should note that most Texans in those days ignored the speed limit signs. If a sign said 70 miles per hour, the drivers would zoom down the road at 85-90. So, on that snowy day, as I went out of the main gate of Chase Field on my way home, I immediately noticed cars that had slid off the road into ditches. I saw over five cars that had crashed into poles or slid into ditches during my 10 minute drive home. Only a half inch of snow! Really? The people here had no idea you should slow down and be a little more cautious when there was snow on the ground. It was crazy.

Spun Out

In January 1974, before purchasing my Mobile Traveler, I took eight days leave and drove my Volkswagen Kombi to Creve Coeur, Missouri (just west of Saint Louis) to meet up with my old doctor friend George and another friend Rodney, just to visit and have some jam sessions. George lived next door to me when I was in Pensacola and was a drummer and Rodney played the bass. They had their instruments and I brought my guitar and amplifier. It was a great time. However, it snowed several times while I was there, so I decided to leave a day early. The night before I left, it snowed some more … six to eight inches. So, in the morning I put chains on the rear tires of my Kombi and cautiously headed out for Texas.

As I was heading southwest on Route 44, the weather cleared, and the roads improved. After a few hours, I didn't feel like I needed the chains anymore, so I stopped and took them off. When driving with chains, you have to keep your speed somewhat lower. Now without the chains I could push up to the speed limit and make better time.

When I got started again, the road seemed clear with only occasional patches of snow which I could slow down to pass over. Then I hit a long patch of black ice, which I didn't see coming. I started skidding, and unfortunately, I touched the brakes to slow down. Mistake! The Kombi immediately spun to the left so that I ended up driving backwards on the ice with my car in forward gear. I vividly remember seeing the man's face in the car behind me as our cars faced each other…him going forward, me going backwards. He looked extremely frightened, with eyes wide as saucers. I touched the brakes again. Why did you do that, Marty? Around I went for another 180 degrees to the left, only this time I continued skidding into a ditch on the median side of the road at about 30 m.p.h.

The Kombi hit the snowbank in the median and rolled over. My wheels were straight up, my amp and guitar had crashed into the roof of my car and I was hanging upside down in my seat belt. Fortunately, I was OK … just a few bruises and a rapidly palpitating heart.

Most of the cars around me had slowed down and several stopped to help me. It was amazing how responsive the people were. We pushed my Kombi upright and one man with a truck and a rope pulled me out of the ditch onto the road. Amazingly, my camper was undamaged (just a few scratches) and started right up. Boy! Was I lucky! I noticed a restaurant at the next exit and offered to buy anyone lunch or coffee. I didn't know how else to show my gratitude to the 10-15 people that had stopped to help me. I drove to the restaurant, but no one took me up on my offer. So, after a short while, I left and was once again on my way home, with a cautious eye out for black ice. I made it back to Beeville with no further incidents.

Mexico

A group of adventurous pilots from VT-26 decided to take a trip to the Mexican mountains to do some trail motorcycle riding. We all applied for ten days leave and were soon on our way. I had built a motorcycle trailer out of an old boat trailer. I could put two motorcycles on that. Another guy had a trailer as well. So, with three cars, two trailers and three motorcycles, seven of us headed off to Mexico.

The first day we traveled to McAllen, Texas, where we were processed through Mexican Customs. Once we had all finished the paperwork there, we gassed up our cars and motorcycles and headed out Route 40D for Monterrey. The speed limit sign said 100. Wow!! One hundred. There was no way my Mobile Traveler was going to do 100, especially hauling a trailer. Looking a little closer, I noticed the signs said 100 k.p.h. "KPH" for kilometers per hour. That made more sense. One hundred KPH was about 65 MPH.

Monterrey was about 150 miles to the west of McAllen. We made the trip in about three hours. After our travels, we decided to stop for dinner and spend the night at a Holiday Inn in Monterrey. I never realized there were Holiday Inns in Mexico. After a great meal and a good night's sleep, we were on our way again.

Our caravan continued west for about 30 miles on Highway 40D to Saltillo, where we stopped to do a little shopping and sightseeing. By now, we were really in Mexico. Very few people spoke English. So, it was kind of fun, using the Spanish that I had learned in high school to communicate with native Mexicans. I'm sure that they got a chuckle or two from my attempts to speak their language. While we were shopping, I asked a group of Mexican boys to watch our motorcycles. I thought I told them, with my high school Spanish, that I would pay them some money to do that, but when they doubled over laughing, I realized that I must have said something completely different.

One of the guys in our group was married to a Mexican, a wonderful lady who made the trip with us. Her name was Maria and she was our "go-to" person if we had any culture questions. She was fluent in Spanish. I told her what I said to the boys (in what I thought was Spanish) and she immediately blushed and turned away from me. I asked her, "Well, what did I say?" She had a hard time telling me, but finally said it was very vulgar. I realized I didn't know Spanish as well as I thought, and I had better be more careful in the days ahead.

We continued our trip by heading south for another 120 miles to a little town called Matehuela, which was our final destination in the cars. That night, seven of us went to a local restaurant for an authentic Mexican dinner. I loved Mexican food and was looking forward to this. I was thinking "I know what a burrito is. I know what a taco is. I know what a tortilla is. I should be in good shape." I was sitting next to Maria, so I knew I could check with her about any additional language issues that I might have.

When the menus came, I was able to select some things that I knew I liked. So far, so good. After we had all ordered, the waitress brought what I guessed were bowls of appetizers to our table. Some of the bowls had green jalapenos in them and some other bowls had circular slices of carrots in them. The guys at the table jumped in and started eating the jalapenos. I knew what they were. I imagined that in Mexico they would really be hot. They were. The guys were fanning their mouths and drinking water. I had to laugh. I thought to myself, "I think I'll stick to the carrots. They look safe." So, I took one and as it was making its trip to my mouth, Maria said something to me and tried to grab my arm.

Too late! It was in my mouth and I had already crunched down one time. It would be a gross understatement to say that it was hot. Water! Water! Fire! Fire! I immediately broke out in a sweat. My mouth was on fire. Did I swallow some of the juice? Oh no! I did. My stomach felt like I swallowed acid. I tried to say something, but my voice didn't work. I couldn't say anything more than "Ahh. Ahh." Maria said, "I tried to stop you. Those are Zanahorias Escabeche (Mexican name for spicy carrots) and are the hottest things on the table. The jalapenos are mild compared to them. You should drink some milk."

She ordered me some "leche" and soon, I was much better and much wiser. No more experiments for me. When my meal came, I asked Maria, "Is this all right? Is that all right?" Only after her approval would I actually eat something.

What a night!

The next morning, we headed to the mountains on three motorcycles and a jeep. This was truly an adventure. We were traveling back roads and trails to a little city in the mountains in a very remote part of

Approaching the Real de Catorce tunnel

Mexico. Real de Catorce was a small mining town on the west side of the mountain range that paralleled our trip from Saltillo the day before.

When we got there, we had the opportunity to tour the town, do some shopping and to experience another authentic Mexican meal in Catorce before turning our bikes around and heading down the mountain back to Matehuela. The next day we headed back to Laredo and then home to Beeville. A trip I will always remember.

Parked outside a restaurant in Real de Catorce

Back to Sea Duty

When I returned to Beeville, it was time to think about my next assignment in the Navy. I had asked for a flying billet for my next at-sea assignment, but the Navy assigned me as ship's company to aircraft carrier *U.S.S. Franklin D. Roosevelt.* I would be the Air Launched Missiles Officer. *Roosevelt* was home ported in Mayport, Florida (just east of Jacksonville), so in October 1975, after two and a half years in Texas, I headed back to the East Coast for my next assignment.

CHAPTER 9

U.S.S. FRANKLIN D. ROOSEVELT (CV-43)

November 1975 – March 1977

Events in the Navy and Worldwide During This Time

January 21, 1976
The first commercial Concorde flight.

July 18, 1976
Nadia Comaneci earned 7 perfect scores of 10 at the 1976 Summer Olympics.

January 3, 1977
Apple Computer was incorporated.

January 12, 1977
U.S.S. Franklin D. Roosevelt collided with the Liberian freighter *Oceanus* while transiting the Strait of Messina.

January 20, 1977
    Jimmy Carter became the 39th President of the United States.

January 21, 1977
    U.S. President Jimmy Carter pardoned Vietnam War draft evaders.

Norfolk

Before reporting to *U.S.S. Franklin D. Roosevelt*, I had to undergo…. guess what. More training. I left Beeville in October 1975 and reported to Naval Air Station Norfolk, Virginia on November 3 for the first of two classes I needed before reporting to *Roosevelt*. The first class was a two-week overview of Air Launched Weapons (ALW). Since my primary billet was Air Launched Missiles Officer, it seemed logical that I should know more about these weapons.

After completing the ALW course, I began a class for Officers of the Deck (O.O.D.). I knew I would be expected to qualify as an Officer of the Deck on *Roosevelt*. The Officer of the Deck (Underway) was responsible for the normal operation of the ship at sea when the captain wasn't on the bridge or when he was on bridge and gave the O.O.D. that responsibility under his guidance. Ultimately, the captain was still in charge, but authority to make decisions in his absence or while he was asleep was given to another officer, normally the O.O.D. If any kind of danger was imminent, the O.O.D. would act as appropriate and then immediately contact the captain for instructions about what to do.

This was an important responsibility, since the safety of the entire crew of 5000 men depended on good decisions by the Captain and his O.O.D.s. So, I focused a lot of energy on learning about systems on a carrier, a ship's external lighting, the Rules of the Road on the ocean and inland waters, and navigation.

After these classes, I left Norfolk and headed to Florida and on December 2, 1975, I reported to *U.S.S. Franklin D. Roosevelt* in Mayport,

Florida. At that time, *Roosevelt* was undergoing some extensive repairs and wouldn't be getting underway for several months.

San Pablo

Since we would be in port for nine to ten months, it seemed like my first order of business should be finding a place to live, hopefully not too far from Mayport. I couldn't find an apartment that I liked in Mayport, so I continued my search a few miles south and found a nice place at the San Pablo Apartments. I signed up for an end apartment since I had my guitars and amplifiers with me and planned to use them. I could put the amps on the outside wall, so no one would be disturbed when I cranked them up. This worked pretty well and was even better since at the time, there was no one living in the apartment on the other side either. A pretty nice buffer.

One day when I returned to my apartment after jogging, I met the two young ladies (Mary Lou and Mary), who lived in the apartment next to the vacant one. It was nice to meet some people in the complex and they both were about my age. Being single, it was always nice to meet other singles, which I assumed they were.

During the subsequent weeks, I dated Mary Lou a few times, but it didn't take long for me to realize that my eyes were really on Mary. I wanted to ask her out but that was obviously a bit tricky since she and Mary Lou shared an apartment. So, I asked them both out. We would go out as a threesome to various restaurants. Eventually, I got to know Mary and wanted to take her out without Mary Lou tagging along.

On one of our threesomes, we got into a discussion about religion. Mary Lou said she was a Catholic. Mary said she was Protestant. That was it! I said I was Protestant as well and asked Mary about her church. After she told me about her church, Christian Center in Jacksonville Beach, I said Christian Center sounded interesting and asked her if it would be OK for me to accompany her on Sunday. She said yes. Alone at last.

Christian Center

I had drifted away from going to church during the past few years, so I didn't exactly know what to expect. But if Mary went there, it would be all right. What I didn't know was that Christian Center was a very lively Charismatic church. I grew up going to an Episcopal church which was very different, very stoic.

Christian Center was three blocks from the ocean and when Mary and I drove up to the building, I noticed several surf boards leaning against it. That was cool. The surfers probably do some surfing in the morning before church and then head back out afterwards. The service would likely be very informal.

When we entered the church, which was not very large, the first guy I met was a big burly fellow who welcomed me with a bear hug. Now, I wasn't the kind of guy who went around hugging other men. So, in my head, I was saying, "Whoa, wait just a minute. Let me out of here. Where's my car?", but my feet kept moving straight ahead. I was with Mary and that guy was behind me now. I made a mental note to avoid going near him when the service was over.

The service was very friendly, and the pastor's name was Larry Carson. Everybody called him Parson Carson. I enjoyed the service and Parson's sermon was very interesting and easy to understand. So, I decided that I would come back again the next week. Soon, I was a regular. Then a few weeks later, while Parson was preaching, I realized I wanted to rededicate my life to God. I wasn't really sure if I had ever done that the first time. During the service, Parson said something like, "I think someone here is ready to commit their life to Christ. If that's you, just stand up." That was it! I was up without even thinking about it. Then I noticed that another guy stood up also. I thought, maybe I wasn't fast enough and started to sit back down. Parson chuckled and said, "That's OK. It's for the both of you." Then he prayed for us. Whew! That was great. I was so happy, that I even hugged the "bear hug" guy as I left that day.

Another Car

Car #9 - 1976 Fiat 124 Spider -- In January 1976, I decided to get another Fiat. I had traded in my mustard yellow Fiat and had recently realized how much I really liked it, so I got another one, just like it, only this one was green and a few years newer.

Pre-Cruise Preparations

Repairs to the ship had gone quickly. In March, we would begin sea trials and preparations for our Mediterranean Cruise. First on our schedule of preparations was a Fast Cruise. When first I heard that term, I thought it would be a sea period that was over quickly. However, I learned that "fast" meant tied up to the pier. We had a five day Fast Cruise. For five days no one left the ship. It was as if we were at sea. We ran drills, stood watches, moved weapons around, things we would normally do when we were underway and operational. From time to time, some of the wives dropped by the parking lots and waved to their husbands onboard. That must have been hard for both of them. After five days of this, the whole crew was ready for some liberty.

During that week, while we were tied up at Mayport, a major weather front came through. I was on the bridge, simulating an underway watch, when three small tornados touched down simultaneously in Mayport. As they crossed the Saint Johns River they turned into waterspouts. They weren't very large, but they came within a half mile of the ship and they were definitely tornadoes. A real exciting moment.

Flying

My orders to *Roosevelt* included a clause stating I would be flying. Proficiency flying … which was defined as four flight hours per month. That was not very much in my opinion since the aircraft that the ship used were propeller driven and one flight could be four hours. In my thinking, one flight each month couldn't be called proficiency. The primary aircraft we flew was the Grumman C-1 Trader. It had two engines and was used to bring supplies and mail aboard the ship while we were underway. When we were in port it was used to get supplies and repair parts from other airfields. These were the missions I was scheduled to fly. I was only qualified to fly "right seat" which is the co-pilot chair. The pilot-in-command sat in the left seat. I never qualified as pilot-in-command and never got to land the C-1 on the carrier.

I also flew the Piper U-11 Aztec on a supply mission south from Mayport to Marathon, Florida for a part pickup. Again, I was "right seat." This flight took over three hours each way between Marathon, Florida and Mayport. This one flight made me proficient for that month. Really?

After *Roosevelt* got underway for the Mediterranean Sea, I never flew the C-1 or U-11 again. The flying part of my orders was changed. However, I did still get my flight pay. So, I didn't complain too much. I was looking forward to flying in Europe during the upcoming cruise, but that never happened either.

Engaged

Mary and I continued going to Christian Center and eventually I got up the nerve to ask her out on a date. I had tickets to The Who concert at the Gator Bowl in Jacksonville in August. So, I asked her if she would want to go. I didn't think she was big on rock concerts and certainly not a Who fan. So, I was quite surprised when she said "yes."

On August 7, 1976, we went to the concert. It was an all- day affair with several other groups performing before The Who. We sat on a blanket on the grass and enjoyed each other's company for the entire day. Mary commented to me that the air smelled funny. I

Marty and Mary outside my Mobile Traveler

knew that the smell was marijuana. It was thick. When it got dark and the lights came on, you could actually see a smoke cloud hovering over the field. In spite of the marijuana, we had a great time on our first date.

We continued to see each other for the rest of the month and in September, I asked her to marry me. Again, I was surprised that she said "yes." I took ten days leave in September so Mary and I could drive my Mobile Traveler camper up to Maryland to meet my mom and dad. Then we drove around some tourist spots in Pennsylvania before heading back home to Jacksonville.

Underway

On October 3, 1976, *Roosevelt* got underway for the Mediterranean. It was hard to leave Mary. We knew letters would be our main communication during the next few months … no face to face communication until December. We had set the time for our wedding to be during my Christmas leave. We didn't know exactly when that would be, but I thought, "Surely we will be in port somewhere during Christmas and surely I would be allowed to take leave to come home to get married." But it was a little too early to plan my travel details, since *Roosevelt* would make several other port calls before then.

Our first port call was Rota, Spain. After transiting the Atlantic Ocean, we pulled into Rota to refuel and resupply. Soon we were back at sea, through the Straits of Gibraltar and into the Med.

Fuel in the Water

Roosevelt was an old ship and almost immediately she started experiencing maintenance difficulties. Jet aircraft fuel was called JP5 and the ship had to have a lot of it to refuel the jets in the air wing. The JP5 was kept cool by running the JP5 pipes through the ship's cold fresh water pipes. That's right. One pipe inside the other. The JP5 pipes were old and leaky, so our fresh water supply had a small amount of jet fuel in it. The water was safe to drink but you could smell the JP5 in it.

Because a small amount of JP5 in the water was not harmful, nothing much was done about it. The ongoing joke was to have a sign near a water fountain that said, "No Smoking within 50 feet."

Air Launched Missiles (AM) Division

I was the division officer for the AM Division, responsible for the storage, care, preparation and transportation of Air Launched Missiles on *Roosevelt*. As a rotating assignment, one of the 18 men assigned to the AM Division was on watch during all off-duty times. The man on watch had the simple task of answering the phones and making sure that no equipment disappeared from the AM work space while the crew was off-duty. It was a boring watch and most of the guys would read or see what was on the ship-wide TV during their overnight watch time. It was also their responsibility to have coffee ready when the crew reported for work for the next shift.

Each man in the shop had a personalized coffee mug. All of the mugs for the division were hung on a board next to the coffee pot. Some of them looked like they had coffee crust in them from previous cruises. They looked disgusting and unsanitary, but the guys didn't seem to care. As a matter of fact, they seem to take pride in the nastiness of their mugs.

In December, a new enlisted man was assigned to the AM Division. Airman Sharpe was 18 years old and had just joined the Navy and wanted to make a good impression on his new shipmates. Being the most junior enlisted man in the division, he was soon given an overnight watch. In the morning, when the crew reported for work, the AM spaces were immaculate, perfectly cleaned and spotless. He had been busy. The coffee was made but, unfortunately for Sharpe, he had cleaned the coffee mug board and it was also spotless and he had cleaned everyone's dirty mug. The crud on the inside that the owners were so proud of was gone. These mugs looked brand new. In spite of the great job he had done otherwise, everyone's attention was on their mug and they let Sharpe know that they were not happy. Sharpe's efforts to please had backfired. I felt really sorry for him. He had tried so hard to make a good impression.

Later that morning, I called him into my office and thanked him for his hard work during the night, but I don't think that helped him much.

Drugs in the Magazines

In the 1970's, drugs were a big attraction for young men in their late teens and early twenties. Marijuana and PCP were very popular. These drugs were obviously illegal, but nonetheless, many enlisted guys still used them, but not so much on the ship. Alcohol was also not allowed onboard. In their free time onboard, some guys looked for other outlets, but there really weren't any as attractive to them as drugs and alcohol. So, some of these young sailors looked for places where they could use the drugs or drink the booze that they had smuggled aboard. But there just weren't many good hiding places on an aircraft carrier.

One day in late January, my division chief came to me and told me that one of our men was caught smoking dope (slang for marijuana). When I asked the chief for the details, he took me to one of our missile storage magazines. These compartments were kept locked for obvious reasons, but all of the men in the AM Division had access to the key. Smoking was not allowed anywhere near these ammunition magazines. Missiles are obviously highly explosive. The chief showed me where the man had been smoking the marijuana. Right next to an AIM-9 Sidewinder missile. There was a small pile of ash and marijuana residue on the floor where he had hastily tried to conceal his sin, but he had been caught in the act. The smoke and marijuana smell were still in the magazine. There was no doubt. I couldn't believe that he had done that. What was he using for brains? What was he thinking? He could have been killed.

The airman was arrested and put in the brig. Shortly thereafter he waived his rights to a trial and accepted the captain's N.J.P (Non-Judicial Punishment) which was reduction in rank, forfeiture of pay, and four months in the brig. He was returned to the United States to serve his prison term. I saw him one more time in Jacksonville in March. He was raking a grassy area with some other prisoners. The marine guards watching the prisoners would not let me speak with him. That was the last time I saw him.

Ports of Call

About once each month, *Roosevelt* would go into a port and the men aboard would have the opportunity to have some shore liberty in a foreign country. We were all looking forward to some of the great liberty spots in the "Med" but mostly we went to Naples, which got pretty old after one or two times. Naples did have some nice restaurants but not much else there attracted me. So, I used my liberty to go to Naval Support Activity (N.S.A.) Naples, an American facility where there was a gym and a movie theater.

It was about an eight-mile cab ride from the dock (Fleet Landing) to N.S.A. Naples. This was where I learned how you are supposed to drive in Italy. The roads were congested and everyone's way of dealing with that was to lean on the horn. The cab drivers and just about everyone else drove around with one hand on the wheel and the other on the horn. It didn't really help the congestion, but it seemed to help the drivers.

One of the nice liberty ports that we visited was Catania, Sicily. The ship anchored on the eastern side of Sicily. We could see Mount Etna (an active volcano) from the flight deck of the ship. A short 15 minute boat ride from the ship and we were at the docks of Catania. It seemed like most every port in Italy had a U.S. navy base nearby. Catania was no exception. About 10 miles inland was Naval Air Station Sigonella, which turned out to be a good place to hang out for liberty. Catania itself was also pretty cool. There were many authentic Italian restaurants and tourist spots. I learned a few things about Italian food in Catania. Spaghetti was not a main dish but a side dish to go with other foods. I never saw pizza on the menu at all. I might have missed it, but I never noticed it. The food was really good though: lasagna, tortellini, ravioli, vermicelli, cacciatore, and cannelloni. Just about everything was pasta oriented, but this authentic Italian food just tasted great.

December Wedding

During the early part of the cruise, my highest off-duty priority was working out wedding plans. Mary and I both thought it would be neat to get married in England. We could have each flown into London, gotten married and had our honeymoon, all right there in England. However, that didn't work out. There were some residency and religion issues that we didn't have time to resolve. So, it was on to Plan B, which was to be married in Jacksonville.

I had requested three weeks leave during *Roosevelt's* in- port period over Christmas. But the leave request approval was taking an exceptionally long time. Was someone holding it up? Did they need more information? Had I made someone angry? Was I in trouble? I needed to plan a flight to the US and there wasn't much time. Eventually, I found out that the issue was that I would miss some at-sea time if I took three weeks leave. I didn't think that should be an issue, since my division chief was one of the best on board. Finally, I went to the Executive Officer (second in command) to ask him what could be done to speed up the process. He said he would take care of it. The next day I had the approval.

We anchored in Taranto, Italy in mid-December. I was on the first liberty boat ashore and caught a cab to the Taranto train station. There were four of us trying to get to Rome for international flights to the United States. At the train station ticket window, we were told the train to Rome was currently loading on Track Eleven. So, we got our train tickets and hustled to Track Eleven. We saw a train waiting there, so we climbed aboard. No one took our ticket and there was no one else in the car we were in. I guess we should have been suspicious, but I wasn't. Italy was a strange place with unusual ways of doing things. I thought this was going to be a nice, quiet and spacious trip. We waited for about ten minutes for the train to get going, when one of the guys went to look for something to eat for the trip.

Soon, he came running towards us waving his hands and shouting, "Wrong train! Wrong train! Our train is on Track Nine!" We all scrambled to get our suitcases and get to Track Nine. We managed to get aboard just as the train began moving. We almost missed it. The next train to Rome wouldn't leave until the next day. That would have been a disaster.

We must have gotten the local train because it stopped for passengers about every 20 minutes. The 250 mile trip to Rome should have taken about four hours, but not today. It took us nearly eight hours to get to Rome. We were all worried about our flights. Would we be too late? Would we have to reschedule? Go stand-by?

When we got to the Rome train station, we jumped in two cabs and went right to the airport. We checked in with our respective airlines. I was the only one who had missed his flight. I was able to book a flight for the next morning. The ticket agent spoke English (thank goodness) and told me that she could also re-ticket my connecting flight from Philadelphia to Jacksonville. She gave me both tickets.

The other three guys all made their flights. They were going to New York. I was going to Philadelphia. I said goodbye to them and checked into a hotel. After a short night, I would be on the early flight to Philadelphia. The next day's early flight wasn't so early after all. The airliner had a maintenance problem and was four hours late leaving, but at last I was on my way to the United States. But now I had another problem. Since we would be four hours late, I would miss my re-ticketed flight from Philadelphia to Jacksonville. Was anything going to go right? The way things were going, I wondered if I would make it to Florida in time for my wedding.

When I got to Philadelphia, I went to the ticket counter to find out when the next flight to Jacksonville would be, since I had missed mine. The ticket agent said, "All of today's flights are full and most of tomorrow's are also." She said, "It's Christmas time and many people are traveling." I was very disappointed to lose another day. It seemed like I was spending my entire leave time traveling or waiting to travel. She asked me if I had a ticket. I showed her the ticket that I got in Rome and she smiled and said, "You've already been rescheduled. You are booked on a flight leaving in about one hour." Yaaaaa-whoooo!

I had no idea how that happened, but I was asking no questions. I called Mary to let her know when I would be in Florida and was soon on the final leg of my trip. Jacksonville – here I come!

The timing was perfect, because in Florida, by law, you had to get your marriage license at least three days prior to your wedding. I arrived in Jacksonville late on the 16th, we got our license the next day, exactly three days prior to the 20th - the date of our wedding. At 12 o'clock noon on December 20th, 1976, Mary and I were married in her home in Jacksonville. Mary's sister Sydney was the Matron of Honor, and Sydney's husband, Vinny, was my Best Man. Parson Carson officiated the wedding. It was so wonderful that my mother was able to be there as well. No one from *Roosevelt* was able to come and none of my other relatives were able to make it to Florida either. I guess I didn't mind too much. I was so happy to be home and with Mary again.

Honeymoon

Mary had planned the wedding and I planned the honeymoon. For the first leg of our honeymoon, we had tickets for a flight out of Jacksonville at 5 PM that evening. So, after a short, small reception, we jumped into our limo, which was a pink Cadillac that belonged to Mary's sister. She was a Mary Kay Consultant. We hadn't gotten too far when another car intercepted us. It was Mary's Aunt Ellen. She got out and handed me an envelope. "Did you forget something?" The envelope had our airline tickets. I had left them back at Mary's parent's house. Boy, was I in a fog! Our flight from Jacksonville to Kennedy in New York went smoothly. In New York, we got a bus from Kennedy to La Guardia. Then at La Guardia, we got on a smaller airplane that took us to Burlington, Vermont.

It was nearly eleven PM when we got to Burlington. The next leg of our trip was to be by car. We were picked up by a guy who resembled

Paul Bunyan; big, tall and burly, wearing a flannel shirt and boots. He drove us up the mountain roads at a speed that neither Mary nor I was comfortable with. We just huddled down in the back seat and closed our eyes. He took us right to our lodging at Smuggler's Notch, Vermont. Smuggler's Notch was a skiing resort and Mary was a Florida girl. She had never been skiing before.

The next morning, we left our room in search of a restaurant for breakfast. We found, that there were no restaurants open for breakfast in Smuggler's Notch. None! We did find a little convenience store, so we got some instant coffee and other food items and went back to our room to make our own breakfast. There were no microwaves in those days, so we had to make do with the not-so-hot water out of the faucet. We had warm instant coffee and instant oatmeal. What a great honeymoon breakfast! We didn't mind so much. It was all part of the adventure. We put some ice cream and soda that we bought outside our window, since our room didn't have a refrigerator and the temperature outside was well below freezing. This worked for the ice cream, but the soda bottle was frozen solid when we brought it in later to drink.

Mary had one or two days of ski lessons, before she came down with a terrible cold, or the flu. We weren't sure exactly what it was or how she caught it, but for two days, she felt horrible. Christmas in bed. Blaaahh!

A few days later, we returned to the Burlington airport for the second leg of our honeymoon trip. Mary recounts a story here. She was sitting on a bench waiting for our plane. I was not with her at the moment. There was a PA announcement. The lady said "Mrs. Herzog, Mrs. Herzog, will you please come to the American Airlines ticket counter?" Mary was not used to hearing herself called Mrs. Herzog. She told me later that she wanted to stand on her seat and shout, "That's me!"

From Burlington, we flew back to New York and spent a week exploring the Big Apple before flying back home to Jacksonville. We stayed in the Barbazon Hotel just south of Central Park. Our Itinerary included all the tourist places: Empire State Building, Times Square, Staten Island Ferry, Natural History Museum and Statue of Liberty. Before we knew it, the week was over and we were heading back home.

Another Car

Car #10 1975 Oldsmobile Cutlass - This was Mary's car. It was a real nice comfortable car with plenty of room and plenty of pick-up. I didn't personally drive it very much. It was Mary's transportation.

Back to *Roosevelt*

In early January, after a tearful goodbye, I was on my way back to Europe. I wasn't sure what my future held. I didn't want to be regularly separated from Mary as happens in the Navy. I had applied to be a demonstration pilot with the Blue Angels. That would have been a great assignment. However, I was turned down. Then I found I was not selected for promotion to lieutenant commander with my peers. That was hard to take. My response was to resign from the Navy. I submitted a letter requesting release from the Navy as soon as possible.

The Pinger

Even though I was resigning from the Navy, I wanted to get my "qual" as Officer of the Deck (Underway). I had been working on it for four months and I was nearly there. Each at sea period, watch teams were formed to stand duty on the bridge the entire time *Roosevelt* was underway. There were four to six watch-standers on each team and six watch teams. The boss of each team was the O.O.D.

As I was in training, I worked with different O.O.D.'s each at sea period. One particular O.O.D. was known among the watch-standers as the "Pinger." It seemed like he was always "bouncing off the wall" about something, very excitable and no fun to work for. No quiet moments when he was in charge. He told us, "If you aren't busy 100% of the time then you probably aren't doing your job." Oh Boy!

I worked with the "Pinger" on one at-sea period, after working an at-sea period with LT(jg) Bart Finnegan. Bart was fun to work with. He was jovial and always smiling. He kept us busy, but not 100%

of the time. There were appropriate ways and times to maintain a diligent watch without being intensely overboard about it. Bart was also a prankster. On this at sea period, he conspired with the watch team to play a joke on the "Pinger."

After a few days at sea, on a dark night, Bart told us to keep our vigilance while we stood out of sight at different places on the bridge. The bridge area was kept dark with red lighting, so the watch standers could have the best possible outside visibility, once their eyes had night adapted. When the "Pinger" came on the bridge to take over from Bart, he would see no one on the bridge, even though the full team was there doing their duties. He would have one of those "bounce off the walls" moments. What would he do? How would he act?

When the time came for the "Pinger" to report to the bridge, he showed up and asked the sailors in the after-bridge area (just behind the bridge) where the "Night orders" were. The bridge and after bridge were separated by a wall or bulkhead with a few windows in it so the crew could communicate with the watch team without calling them on the phone. Night orders were standing orders from the Captain during the period of time he was not on the bridge. The Captain was never too far away. Tonight, he was in his at sea cabin, which was just behind the after bridge. The Captain was hopefully getting some much-needed sleep.

The "Pinger" came on to the bridge and his eyes had not night-adapted yet. He looked around and saw no one. "Bart", he called. "Where are you?" "Anyone here?" Now he started to panic, thinking – there's no one on the bridge. Who's driving the ship? We could have a collision with another ship. Are there any contacts on radar? He raced from one side of the bridge to the other. Then he picked up the Captain's phone. Oh no! He was actually going to call the Captain. That would not do. He was about to push the button to buzz the Captain's phone in his at sea cabin when Bart reached out of the darkness and grabbed his wrist. The "Pinger" jumped about 2 feet in the air. "Ahhhh!" he exclaimed. He dropped the Captain's phone and then took a few steps backward to compose himself. We all stepped out of the shadows as if nothing had happened. We were all at our stations doing our appropriate jobs.

The "Pinger" had been "had." That night, he really laid into his watch team, but we already had our laugh. It was one of the hardest nights ever, but it was worth it. Every time members of the team passed each other, we winked and then smiled. The next day, Bart talked with the "Pinger" and told him that he should settle down and treat his team a little more kindly. He actually responded to that counsel and things ran much more smoothly for the rest of the at sea period.

Collision

When I returned from the United States, I met the ship in Naples. We got underway on January 11th, 1977. That night, I was on watch as Officer of the Deck-in training as we approached the Straits of Messina. (between Sicily and mainland Italy). Shortly after midnight, just after being relieved by another O.O.D. and I was down in my stateroom, when I heard the collision alarm – a rapid ringing of an electronic bell. Then I heard over the 1MC (the ship's public address system), "Collision – collision – all hands, take a brace." Then the whole ship shook. I jumped to my feet and ran up to the hangar deck to see if the ship was in danger. It turned out that the ship was safe, but we had to turn around and head back to Naples for two weeks repair in dry-dock.

The story from the O.O.D. on watch was that the ship that we ran into was a Liberian freighter. It was a pitch-black night and the freighter crossed right in front of us, with no lights on. There was no way to avoid the collision. The O.O.D. also said that it appeared that no one was on the freighter's bridge. Strange since this was a very narrow passage and they were traveling at a ninety-degree angle to the main traffic.

Another interesting thing was that one of *Roosevelt's* crew was using the head (bathroom) in one of the forward spaces at the time of the collision. One of the commodes, just aft of where he was, dropped into the sea and the rest of the head (bathroom) was exposed to the outside. I imagine that guy was quite shook up.

Shortly after that, on February 18, 1977, I qualified as Officer of the Deck, Underway on *Roosevelt*. That was a big accomplishment. Only a few junior officers (five or six) on the ship were qualified as O.O.D.,

Underway. The ship's captain called me into his office. He congratulated me on my qualification as O.O.D. and asked me if I was absolutely sure that I still wanted to resign. He had forwarded my letter to the Bureau of Naval Personnel in Washington but could pull it back at any time, if I wanted. I told him, that since I had been passed over for promotion, I thought that I should get a fresh start somewhere else. Then he told me that if I stayed in the Navy, I would surely get promoted the next year and that I was one of the best officers he had onboard. I was really gratified to hear that, but it was all too late for me. I wanted out.

Matterhorn

My last liberty port on *Roosevelt*, prior to being released from the Navy was in Genoa, Italy. A group of us decided to drive from Genoa to Cervinia on the Italian/Swiss border for a skiing trip. How exciting! I had never skied in the Alps before. We drove on highway E-25 across northern Italy to Saint Vincent before heading north on a back road SR-46 to Cervinia. There was no speed limit on the E-25 highway, so we cruised to our turn off quite rapidly...90-100 mph most of the way.

When we got to Cervinia, we checked into a hotel, rented skis and readied ourselves for the next day of skiing.

When I looked out our front window, I saw this majestic mountain peak. It was the Matterhorn. Right on the ski slope.

Our room had two toilets. At least, I thought there were two toilets. However, one of them really looked strange. It had knobs that squirted water up rather than down. I was perplexed. When I mentioned

The Matterhorn

this to one of the guys, he told me it was a water fountain. He really cracked up when I asked him why there was such a low water fountain in the bathroom. Then he told me that this fixture was a bidet (pronounced "bih-day"). It was more like a sink to clean yourself after using the toilet. Never seen such a thing.

The next morning, I was looking forward to a big breakfast before hitting the slopes, but sadly, the hotel only had a continental breakfast, pastries and coffee. At least there was coffee.

Soon, we got aboard a gondola and were on our way to the top of the mountain. From the top, you could see Cervinia, Italy to the south and Zermatt, Switzerland to the north. We considered skiing down into Switzerland, but we wondered about things like passports and lift tickets on the Swiss side. Also, we didn't have any Swiss currency. So, we decided to play it safe and stay on the Italian side of the mountain.

Marty and a friend on the summit at the border between Italy and Switzerland

There was plenty of good skiing space. The slopes, even the mogul slopes, were very wide. Great skiing!

After three days of the best skiing I have ever experienced, we were all really tired. In the late afternoon of the third day, I was alone, coming down a gentle slope and realized I was having a hard time lifting my skis up and the legs they were attached to wouldn't lift up either. They were really sore and tired. I saw what looked like a rabbit hole ahead of me. I could not lift my leg to avoid it. I told my foot to come off the ground, but it just wouldn't. My right ski went right in the hole and waaanng! My forward progress immediately stopped, and my knee popped. There I was on my face, with my left leg and ski pointing down the hill and my right leg and ski in the hole, pointing straight downward. I couldn't move. Finally, I was able to break loose of my skis to sit and rest for about 15 minutes. My knee was throbbing. All I wanted to do now was get down the hill. I was able to get my skis on and gingerly ski slowly down the hill to the road where the hotel was. That was it for me. I was done, but even with my injury, it was a wonderful trip. Lesson learned: Do not ski when you are tired.

Separation

When I returned to *Roosevelt*, I received my separation orders. I was to detach during our next in-port period. Several weeks later, I was on my way home. On March 14th, 1977, I reported to the Personnel Office at Naval Air Station, Jacksonville and was separated from the Navy. After spending nearly ten years in the Navy, I was an unemployed civilian.

CHAPTER 10

BROKEN SERVICE

March 1977 – October 1984

Events in the Navy and Worldwide During this Time

February 22, 1980   Olympics
The United States Olympic Hockey Team defeated the Soviet
Union in 1980 Winter Olympics.

May 18, 1980   Mount Saint Helens
Eruption of Mt. St. Helens killed 57 and caused $3 billion
in damage.

March 30, 1981   President Reagan shot
President Ronald Reagan was shot outside a Washington,
D.C. hotel by John Hinckley, Jr.

Teaching in Jacksonville

After resigning from the Navy, I found myself unemployed for the
first time in my life. So, one of my first orders of business upon returning
to Jacksonville, was to find a job. I didn't have to look too hard. A job
just fell into my lap. One of the math teachers at Southside Junior High

School quit in the middle of the year and the school administration was using substitutes to cover for him. I was qualified to take his place, since my degree from Towson State College was in teaching secondary school mathematics. So, I was interviewed and hired on the spot. Also, Southside's varsity baseball team had no coach assigned. The math teacher that resigned was also the baseball coach. So even though I had no previous experience, I was also offered a supplementary position as varsity baseball coach, which I also accepted since there was a financial stipend for this job.

I was assigned five math classes: two classes of elementary algebra, one class of seventh grade remedial arithmetic and two classes of seventh grade mathematics. Surprisingly, the remedial class was quite enjoyable. The students in this class were well behind the other junior high school students, but they were very enthusiastic. Sadly, many of them didn't even know their multiplication facts (multiplication tables).

I generally started the remedial class each day by drilling multiplication facts. I would ask, "John, what's four times eight?" John would answer, and then I would ask the class, "Is that correct?" They would answer, "Yeeeeees!" or "Noooo!" One day, while I was doing this with my class, I called on a young boy named Paul. Paul was a very likeable boy with an infectious smile. Everybody liked Paul. He was a bit of a clown and we all enjoyed his antics.

I said, "Paul, what's seven times eight?" No answer. I thought that maybe he hadn't heard me or was daydreaming, so I asked him again a little bit louder. "Paul! What's seven times eight?" Still no answer. At this point, I started to get a little steamed. Was he ignoring me? That wouldn't do. I had been an officer in the Navy for nearly ten years and when I asked a question, I expected an answer, even if it was "I don't know."

Paul sat in the last row of seats. It seems like trouble-makers always sit in the last row. I remember in my school days, I always looked for a seat in the back. I don't think I classified Paul as a trouble-maker, but he wasn't answering me. So, I walked about halfway down the aisle and asked the question a third time. Still no reply from Paul. I noticed at this point that his eyes were open, and he was staring straight ahead.

The students in the class were a little uneasy, not knowing whether this was one of Paul's games or not. Was Mister Herzog angry? … I was. I was getting steamed.

I walked all the way to the back row and leaned down so that my face was directly in front of Paul's, about six inches away and asked him one last time, "What's seven times eight?" Paul, looking straight ahead, started leaning to his right. He was falling off his chair. He got to about 45 degrees before he jumped and woke up. He had been asleep with his eyes open. I didn't know that was possible. For a moment, I thought that perhaps he had died right there in my classroom. The class was laughing. They enjoyed the whole thing. I was relieved, but I didn't know whether to laugh with them or be angry. It was funny, so I joined in with the rest of the class and had a good laugh. Classroom tension – gone. As Paul was falling off of his chair, I had visualized the headlines in the evening paper, "Boy Dies of Boredom in Math Class."

In June 1977, I was offered a different teaching assignment at Fletcher High School in Jacksonville Beach. This was a great opportunity, since I wanted to teach high school, not junior high. I should mention here that normally teachers weren't offered positions; they had to apply for them. However, Mary's father was the principal at Fletcher and he offered me the position. It was perfect for me. Without too much personal internal deliberation, I took the job even though I knew I would miss coaching baseball. Our season at Southside had been pretty successful. We won more games than we lost in spite of the rookie coach.

Fletcher was the only community school in Duval County. By community school I mean all the students that attended were residents of Jacksonville Beach, Atlantic Beach or Ponte Vedra (all beach communities). Other schools in the county had students bussed in from all over the county.

Mister Friend, the principal, my father-in-law, and now my boss was well liked and respected by the students and the beach community.

I taught at Fletcher for the next two years. Some supplemental coaching positions came my way as well: Assistant Junior Varsity Football Coach, Assistant Varsity Soccer Coach and Head Baseball Coach. Civilian life wasn't all that bad.

So, I still was a baseball coach. The head coach resigned earlier in the year (actually he took another assignment within the Duval County school system.) He left me with a very good team which won the conference title. Unfortunately, that's as far as we went, losing to cross city rival school, Paxton, in the regional final.

Coaching Soccer was a new experience for me. I learned a lot under head coach Billy Reynolds. One the players on Fletcher's varsity Soccer team was Edwin Kohn, who was the son of one of the commanding officers I served under in VA-93. He was a commander at that time. Now he was Vice Admiral Rudy Kohn. Small world.

Houses and Cars

When I got home from Europe, after resigning from the Navy, Mary had an apartment picked out for us. We lived at 10990 Beach Boulevard, Jacksonville for seven months, but we soon realized that we wanted our own home. In October 1977, we purchased our first house together in Jacksonville Beach.

House #2 927 North 22nd Street, Jacksonville Beach – purchased in October 1977 for $45,000. This house was really nice – perfect for us, in a wooded neighborhood. Twenty-two blocks from the ocean.

927 North 22nd Street, Jacksonville Beach

At that point in time, we still had my Fiat, the Mobile Traveler and Mary's Oldsmobile. One weekend, I decided that I would give my four-cylinder Fiat a tune-up. That went well. So, I decided to rebuild the carburetor. After all these repairs the Fiat was really "hummin'." So, I decided to rebuild the carburetor on Mary's Oldsmobile. The eight-cylinder Olds' engine was considerably more complicated than the one in my four-cylinder Fiat.

This was when I realized that I was a much better pilot than I was a mechanic. As I disassembled the Oldsmobile carburetor, I noticed that it had a lot more hoses and springs on it than were on the Fiat. I would loosen a screw and … boing. A spring and a screw would fly through the air, sending me on a search mission for the parts that flew off. I tried to remember where everything belonged because I was going to have to reassemble this carburetor after I cleaned everything. Unfortunately, after reassembling this complicated mechanical device, I had a small handful of springs and screws left over. That was not good.

I started the car and it sounded really sick. It was coughing and sputtering. It just wasn't right. I knew why. The numb-minded mechanic (me) had destroyed the carburetor.

So, I took the Olds to an Oldsmobile dealer and confessed to the head mechanic about what I had done, gave him my handful of extra springs and screws, and asked him to take the carburetor apart and reassemble it. But even after repairs by the dealer, the car still didn't run right and sadly we ended up trading it in on another car. I was a failure as a mechanic.

Car #11 1979 Toyota Corolla Wagon – March 1979 - $6500 – traded in Mary's Oldsmobile Cutlass

Car #12 1979 Plymouth Horizon – July 1979 – traded in the Dodge Mobile Traveler

1979 Toyota Corolla Wagon

Naval Reserves

I had been on active duty for nearly ten years. Ten more years and I would have been eligible for retirement. With this thought in mind, I joined the Navy Reserves. As a Lieutenant, there were many billets available. I learned that the more senior you were, the less opportunity there was in the reserves. My first reserve billet was with VA-1074 (Attack Squadron 1074), a squadron that flew A-7s, the same aircraft that I had flown in the fleet. This billet was wonderful. I was flying again. I had forgotten how much I had missed it.

In the reserves, a unit meets for one weekend each month, and for two continuous weeks some time during the year. The weekend meetings are called "drills." VA-1074 had regular monthly drills, like most every other unit, but there was not enough flying time for each pilot in the squadron during those two days. So, we were granted extra drills at times during the month that were convenient to us. These extra drills were times for the pilots to get their required flight time. There was a financial bonus as well. We received four days' pay for a weekend drill period and two days' pay for extra drills. Not bad.

Just as the captain on *Roosevelt* had predicted, I was promoted to Lieutenant Commander later that year. After that year's promotion cycle, VA-1074 had a large number of Lieutenant Commanders. Even though I was now more senior, I was able to keep a flying billet for a while. But in September 1980, along with several other Lieutenant Commanders, I was detached from VA-1074 and sent to VTU-7474 (Volunteer Training Unit 7474), which was a no-pay unit for officers who didn't have a billet. That was the end of my reserve flying. They had taken my billet away because I was too senior. In VTU-7474, we still had monthly drills, but no real assignment and no pay. It seemed like a waste of time. In a no-pay unit, an officer was still required to attend monthly drill weekends, which counted toward the 20 year time requirement for retirement. However, there was no financial compensation and no real job to do, except during the annual two weeks of active duty.

Two months later, in December 1980, I found a billet in CVW-274 (Carrier Air Wing 274) for L.S.O.s (Landing Signal Officers,) that I was qualified for. This was a half-pay billet with monthly drills where we could work on our L.S.O. skills by working with pilots using simulators. Half-pay actually meant that I received two days' pay for a weekend drill period instead of four. There was a good amount of unscheduled time in this billet, so I had time to read up on naval activities and news. It was during this admin time that I noticed a message that the United States Naval Academy was looking for mathematics instructors from the fleet and reserves. So, I applied and several months later was accepted.

In May 1981, Mary and I packed up and headed for my new full-time active duty assignment in Annapolis, Maryland.

Naval Academy

Now I was to be a university level mathematics instructor, but it had been fourteen years since I graduated from Towson State College. I was surprised at how quickly I forgot what I had learned in college. I had to spend May, June, and July getting caught up and ready for my classes in August.

July 1, 1981 was "I – day" for the class of 1985 (Induction Day). On I – day, the incoming class of plebes reported for duty and was inducted into the Navy. They spent the next six weeks getting acclimated to the Navy and the Naval Academy. Then in late August they turned their focus toward the classroom for the academic year. Some of

United States Naval Academy graduation Class of 1982

these newly inducted midshipmen were to be my first students.

Houses, Cars and Children

When Mary and I first arrived in Annapolis, we were assigned a town house on the base.

12C Sellers Road, Annapolis. We stayed there for about one year. It was really nice being so close to work and the Navy facilities that we used were great: the hospital, the Commissary, and the Navy Exchange. The housing was free to us: no rent, no electricity bills, no water bills, and

*12C Sellers Road, Annapolis
Back door*

no maintenance expenses. Navy officers have the choice of getting a housing supplement in their pay or getting free housing on the base.

After a time, I realized that the housing supplement was a better idea because we could use the extra money to buy a house that we would actually own. That's what we decided to do. We began our search for a home in the Annapolis area and soon found one that was perfect for us.

House #3 1356 Moyer Court, Annapolis

We were home owners again.

1356 Moyer Road, Annapolis

We also purchased a new car during this time.

Car #13 1981 Volvo 2D – $5000

1981 Volvo 2D

Mary and I wanted children and we ended up with five wonderful children.

Child #1 Kevin
"Ski"

June 16, 1979

Kevin

Child #2 Elizabeth
"Libiss"

February 12, 1983

Elizabeth

More Broken Service

In the summer of 1984, my three-year period of active duty at the Naval Academy was complete and I was due for new orders. I began negotiating with my detailer in May. A detailer was an officer working with the Bureau of Naval Personnel, whose job was to match available officers with available jobs. The idea was to give officers assignments that would fit their career path. Sometimes that just wasn't possible.

He offered me a position as a weapons test pilot flying the F/A-18 Hornet in Albuquerque, New Mexico. I was elated. What a great job that would be! However, the commanding officer in Albuquerque turned me down since I didn't have recent fleet experience. Bummer!

Then the detailer said I would be ordered to VC-5 (Composite Squadron Five) in Cubi Point, Philippines, flying the A-4 Skyhawk.

That sounded OK to me, except that there was considerable unrest in the Philippines at that time. Benigno Aquino, a prominent Philippine leader, had recently been assassinated at the Manila Airport and Ferdinand Marcos' leadership position was tenuous. I didn't want to take my family to a dangerous country. When I told the detailer that I didn't like the orders, he told me that if I didn't accept the orders I would have to resign. So, in October 1984, I turned down the orders and resigned a second time. Once again – I was unemployed.

CHAPTER 11

NAVAL STATION KEFLAVIK, ICELAND

November 1984 – October 1989

Events in the Navy and Worldwide During this Time

January 28, 1986

Space Shuttle Challenger disintegrated 73 seconds after launch, killing the crew of 7 astronauts.

April 26, 1986

A mishandled safety test at the Chernobyl Nuclear Power Plant caused the death of over 4000 people.

January 20, 1989

George H. W. Bush succeeded Ronald Reagan as the 41st President of the United States of America.

March 24, 1989

The Exxon Valdez spilled 240,000 barrels of oil after running aground in Alaska's Prince William Sound

---

Civilian Employment

After my second resignation from the Navy, I was only unemployed for a few weeks. One of the professors at the Naval Academy fell down on a stairway near her office and was injured and unable to complete the fall semester. So, I was offered her classes as a temporary seven-week appointment (November 15, 1984 through January 3, 1985).

I was back in the classroom at the Naval Academy teaching Differential Equations.

Realizing that this appointment at the Naval Academy would be temporary, I applied to other colleges for employment and was offered a position as an Assistant Professor at Anne Arundel Community College teaching Computer Science classes and working on a software project. At the end of my first semester there, I applied for a position, as a Department Chairman and after a few interviews, I was accepted by the selection committee. However, the college dean overseeing hiring for the position wanted a larger pool of candidates, so my approval was put on hold.

In the meantime, I was offered an appointment back at the Naval Academy in the Language Department as a computer program designer (Research Assistant Professor). This involved a significant raise so I took the position before the Dean at Anne Arundel Community College made his decision about the chairmanship. I worked in the Language Department at the Naval Academy for just over a year, from June 17, 1985 through August 10, 1986

Keflavik

On November 10, 1984, after my active duty with the Naval Academy was over, I rejoined the reserves, in order to gain more reserve time towards retirement. I found a half pay unit at the Naval Auxiliary Facility Washington which was located at Andrews Air Force Base ... NAVSTA Keflavik 1066 (Naval Station Keflavik 1066). This unit, if mobilized, would transfer as a group to Naval Air Station Keflavik in

Iceland to run the base, administratively, freeing up the permanently assigned officers there to do other operational duties.

As part of our billets, approximately fifty reservists performed our annual two weeks of active duty by flying to Iceland and actually working in our mobilization assignments.  This annual active duty was routinely scheduled in June each year. During my time with NAVSTA Keflavik 1066, I flew to Iceland twice, in June 1985 and June 1986 to be the Station Administrative Officer for two weeks.

Iceland, the Land of Fire and Ice

Iceland was really neat. It's called the Land of Fire and Ice because the region is continually in a state of geological unrest. There are countless geysers, hot springs, mountains, volcanos and glaciers.

Summer time in Iceland was a unique time. The temperature rose into the seventies during the day and went down below freezing at night. So, we wore parkas to work and went back to our quarters in short sleeves at night after work. Since we were so far north, the sun didn't set until sometime around midnight. Because of the late sunset, in order to sleep at night, we would have to close a set of heavy blackout curtains in our rooms to get some darkness.

Even though the sun set around 12 AM, it never really got completely dark. Sunrise was around 3 AM. For a bit of novelty, during the weekend between our two weeks of active duty, we decided to play a midnight softball game with no lights. Very interesting.

There was always a strong breeze in Keflavik, since the base was located on the south western coastline of Iceland and picked up a heavy sea breeze. During the winter time, when it was dark for nearly 20 hours each day, the wind was consistently 30-35 mph. Sometimes the winds were even higher. Cars would have to be parked into the wind so that the doors could be opened and closed with having them blown off.

Geyser about to erupt.

The middle weekend of our two weeks of active duty was the time when we could do some sightseeing, if we so desired. I wanted to see some of the geysers and volcanos in Iceland, so I took a tour on that middle Saturday. I was surprised to find that the geysers didn't have fences around them. You could walk right up to them and look down into the hole from which the boiling hot water would erupt. When you saw the water level rising, you would have to back up quickly to avoid getting wet and burnt during the eruption. That would never do in the United States.

Erupting geyser

Blue Noses

Another Navy tradition similar to becoming a Shellback when you first cross the equator, is becoming a Blue Nose when you cross the Arctic Circle. Each of us had the opportunity to fly in a P-3 Orion north about fifty miles to the Arctic Circle and then back to Keflavik. On the way back the crew of the P-3 got a magic marker and "painted" our noses blue ... part of the tradition. Of course, the first thing we wanted to do when we got back on the ground was to clean our noses.

Three new Blue Noses

Iceland Police

Most Icelandic policemen were big fellows, muscular and strong. They were

Cleaning up

very effective and pretty intimidating. They were not armed – carried no weapons at all. They didn't really need to.

In Iceland there was a zero tolerance to drinking and driving. The rules were simple. If you drank any alcohol at all, you didn't drive. If you were behind the wheel and the police thought you had been drinking, off to jail you went. No questions. No arguments.

One night, while we were in Keflavik, a group of us went to the Officer's Club. I was the designated driver. Knowing the Iceland laws, I had no alcohol at all.

As we gathered to leave, we all climbed in our little four door sedan to head back to officer's quarters. It was pretty chilly, so as I got behind the wheel, I made sure that my window was completely rolled up. As I started the engine, I was quite surprised to see a policeman's face looking in. Where did he come from? What did he want? He gave me a signal to roll down my window and indicated that I should stay in the car. He was a big guy so I was a bit unnerved. All four of us were seated, ready to head to our quarters. After the window was down, he asked me (in English) if I had been drinking. I said, "No." Then he stuck his head in the window directly in front of my head and took a big sniff. Satisfied, he removed his head from the car and gave me the OK sign with his thumb and first finger and left. A very unusual encounter.

I guessed that was the way they did things in Iceland.

40 Years Old

Come on. Nobody's that old.

When I turned forty, a group of men and women from our church threw a gag party for me. They all dressed up to look like they were much older and came to our regular mid-week meeting dressed that way. When I got there, they told me that I didn't have to dress up because I already looked the part. They told a lot of jokes about being old and

Birthday Party

forgetful and gave me some gag gifts, like Geritol and vitamins. A great evening, we all had a ball.

Marine Corps Marathon

Nearly three years later, I ran in the Marine Corps Marathon in Washington D.C. The training for this event took me nearly six months. I ran four to six miles every day during my lunch break and then joined with Moore's Marines for Saturday runs that were longer and supported by some wonderful enthusiastic folks who planned the route and the water stops. Colonel Moore was an elderly man, retired from the Marine Corps and an avid runner. He formed a group affiliated with the Annapolis Striders that prepared novice Marathoners for their first race. That was me. After this preparation, I was able to complete my first (and only) marathon in October 1988.

1988 Marine Corps Marathon 7 miles and still going strong

1988 Marine Corps Marathon Completed - 26.2 miles

Cars and Children

Child #3 MaLisa
"Twinkie"

November 25, 1985

MaLisa

Child #4 Maryel
"Peanut"

July, 7, 1986

Maryel

Herzog Family in 1989

Car #14 - 1986 gray Chevy Astro - Now that our family was getting bigger, we needed a bigger car. The Volvo and the Toyota were too small to hold all of us, especially on a trip. We needed an SUV. So, in November 1986, we bought our first of several SUV's.

Promotion

My Commanding Officer from NAVSTA Keflavik 1066 was Captain Flagg. He called me up one night in August 1986 to congratulate me for being selected for promotion to commander. I wondered how he knew that I had been selected when the 1986 list of commander promotions had not been published yet. As I was pondering that, he told me that he was on the Reserve Commander Promotion Selection Board that year and saw my name on the list. Then I realized how nice it was to have friends in high places.

On August 11, 1986, I returned to active duty with the Mathematics Department at the United States Naval Academy and on October 1, 1986, after about a month and a half at the Naval Academy, it was Commander Herzog. I had new insignia (silver oak leaves), new uniform stripes (three stripes) and a new hat (with scrambled eggs on the brim).

In the summer of 1989, after three more years at the Naval Academy, it was time to negotiate with my detailer once again – I only had four years to go until active duty retirement, so this was a very important time for me. I really didn't want to resign a third time, since that would push my retirement date off into the distant future rather than only four years hence.

My detailer had a great set of orders for me, which I accepted without hesitation. I would be the Operations Officer at N.A.S. Kingsville, Texas (Naval Air Station, Kingsville). This billet would put me in a jet again – actually two different jets: the T-2C Buckeye (Flying with Intermediate Flight Students) and the TA-4J Skyhawk (Flying with Advanced Flight Students). What a great opportunity! Flying again after ten years!

CHAPTER 12

NAVAL AIR STATION KINGSVILLE, TEXAS

November 1989 – July 1991

Events in the Navy and Worldwide During This Time

August 2, 1990   Gulf War
Iraq invaded Kuwait, eventually leading to the Gulf War.

November 7, 1990
Los Angeles Lakers basketball player Magic Johnson announced he had HIV.

Living in Texas

After leaving the Naval Academy, I took my family to Jacksonville, Florida. They stayed with Mary's parents while I went to Water Survival Training at Naval Air Station, Jacksonville for a week. I went through some of the same trainers that I used when I was a student, in addition to a new one that I had never seen before … "The Helo Dunker".

The Helo Dunker was a helicopter body (no rotors or engines) attached to a cable hung over a deep pool. A group of ten water survival students would strap in and then be dropped (a short distance – just a few feet) into the water. The object was for all of us to get out safely. Once the Helo Dunker settled on the bottom, we were to unstrap and then follow each other out either of the two doors (one on each side). We had to do this two times. There were safety divers right there, just in case we had any trouble. This was pretty easy, actually, but then we had to do it a third and fourth time in the dark. That was a bit more exciting. Instead of turning off the lights they gave each of us goggles with the eye panels painted black so that we couldn't see. That way the safety divers still had plenty of light to see us clearly. On the last drop, I ended up being the last pilot to get out (I sat in the very back). This was the most challenging position. They may have put me in that seat because I was the most senior pilot in the group. I only got kicked in the chest one time as the guy ahead of me was trying to swim out. Soon the training was over, and it was time to move on to my new assignment in Texas.

The next week I left Mary and the kids in Florida and drove to Texas to buy the house that Mary and I had agreed on and check in as Operations Officer of Naval Air Station Kingsville. Two weeks later I went back to Florida to get everyone and bring them back to our new home.

House #4 – 1229 West Henrietta Avenue, Kingsville, Texas.

1229 Henrietta Avenue

Hunting

Texas was great hunting country. Once or twice a month some of the guys from the base would go to a ranch belonging to one of their neighbors for a hunt. There was always something to hunt in Texas.

Some of the most fun birds to hunt were Mourning Doves. There were thousands of them on the ranch so getting a good number of them was usually pretty easy. The only problem was that they were very small. When they were cleaned you only had enough meat for two small chicken fingers. So, you needed about eight of them to feed someone. They were really tasty, so we didn't mind and as I already said there was an abundance of them.

The Lease

A good friend of ours in Kingsville offered us a partnership in a huge hunting lease on the King Ranch. As a part of the bargain, we were allowed to harvest (hunt and take) two deer, turkeys, javelina and any other allowable game that we found on the property. In addition, we could place a camper on the property where we could camp anytime we wanted. This trailer became

The Herzog Camper

a weekend retreat for us several times during the hunting season.

At the lease in the evenings, we would often build a campfire and walk around the nearby fields, but that soon changed. One night around sunset, we were walking around, when my friend Charles yelled out to me "Stop!" He had seen some movement near me and slowly approached the area to find an 18-inch rattlesnake a few feet away from me. If I had continued, I would have most certainly been bitten. I never saw the snake until Charles pointed it out to me. It was pretty dark, and I wasn't watching. No more night walks for me. My kids never went back in that field, even in the daylight.

Since the lease was so large, we usually had to drive to where we wanted to hunt. One morning my son, Kevin and I were parked along a trail, hoping to see a deer with big antlers. That never happened, but we did see a line of turkeys crossing the road about 100 yards from where we were. Kevin whispered, "Get one, Dad." I got out of the car and readied myself for a shot.

Normally a turkey would be shot with a shotgun, not a rifle. My 7-millimeter Remington rifle was big enough to bring down a large animal. It was really a bit too much for this medium sized bird. However, it was what I had at the moment and it was way too far for a shotgun anyway. As I was sighting in on the turkey, Kevin whispered to me again, "You better shoot him in the head." "No way," I thought. Are you kidding me? Do I look like Davey Crockett? I would be happy just to hit him, period. So, I shot and hit the turkey dead center in the chest. The bird jumped about six feet into the air and landed. Feathers and bones went everywhere. The gun had removed about two thirds of the bird's right breast. Who knows where all of that went? But we had a turkey dinner that night with the part that remained. It was good.

Another evening activity at the lease was driving around looking for wildlife. One evening we were driving around with Charles and his family when we approached a jackrabbit on the road directly in front of his Suburban. Charles stopped his truck with the rabbit in his headlight beam. The rabbit was transfixed. So, Charles told me to "Shoot him." Everyone else in the car agreed that I should shoot this poor skinny jackrabbit. I thought I was a pretty good shot, so I got my .38 caliber pistol out and carefully aimed while leaning out the right-side window and fired. The rabbit was about 20 feet in front of the car and didn't move when I shot at him. He was perfectly still and yet I missed. How could I miss such an easy shot? I fired two more times and missed both times.

Everyone in the car was laughing and razzing me big time. How embarrassing! Eventually the rabbit looked back at us and simply hopped off the road into the bush and everyone's fun was over. I guess I wasn't such a good shot after all. Do you think the rabbit knew that?

Insects and Spiders

There were all kinds of insects and other pests living in Texas. They seemed to like to congregate close to people's houses. So, every month, we would have our house sprayed to remove them. The next day after spraying, we would find hundreds of dead bugs, beetles and scorpions on the floor in our house and on the ground outside. It's a real wonder none of us ever got bitten or stung by one.

Mary recounts a story about tarantulas. One day she was driving down the road near our house when she came upon a "parade" of tarantulas … hundreds of them, crossing the road from a housing area to a field on the other side of the street. She couldn't avoid them, and it seemed like the parade would never end. There was just no other way to get home so she drove right through them. As she drove along, she remembers the "Crunch, Crunch, Crunch."

Events on the Base

My two summers at Naval Air Station, Kingsville were busy ones. I was responsible for organizing the annual South Texas Airshow at Kingsville. There were a significant number of details to oversee. The first summer, we decided to have a night portion to the airshow. A real novelty. No one at Kingsville recalled ever seeing a night air show before. It was a big success and made some really good money for the Navy Relief Society.

The next year we were able to get the Navy's Flight Demonstration Team, the Blue Angels to perform at our air show. That was a real attraction. More people than ever showed up for the performance.

Unfortunately, during the performance, the Number One plane had a mechanical failure and had to make an emergency landing. Their part of the airshow could not go on without

Blue Angels

the Number One jet, so they all landed and that was that. No Blue Angels. Everyone was so disappointed.

President George Bush was invited to speak at Texas A&I University (later to be Texas A&M), in Kingsville for their commencement ceremony in 1990. There was a significant amount of preparation needed for his trip. For weeks prior, I was working with the university and the secret service to get everyone prepared so that the President's trip would be safe, successful and uneventful. On May 11, 1990, Air Force One flew into Kingsville, to be greeted by much cheering and fanfare,

President George Bush in Kingsville

and even a mariachi band. Soon the President was in his bullet proof car and on his way to the university. The streets of Kingsville were lined with loyal patriotic citizens, waving and cheering. At one point, he actually stopped the caravan and got out to shake hands and greet the people, much to the chagrin of the Secret Service Team. They wanted him to stay safely in the car. The event went off with no problems. After the graduation ceremony, President Bush was back in his plane and on his way to his next stop on Air Force One.

It was kind of funny afterward; I had the impression I knew everything that was going on, but it soon became obvious that I surely didn't. I found out there were Secret Service agents everywhere. One of them was on top of the control tower with a sniper rifle. When I met him, after the President left, my eyes about bugged out. I saw this humongous rifle he was carrying and had to ask him about it. As he was putting it in its case, he told me that he could see everyone on the base from the top of the tower and could have "dropped" anyone who was a threat to the President while he was on the base. The base was big. Some of the shots he was talking about would have been incredible. I was sure that he knew his job.

Soon my assignment at Kingsville was finished and my flying days with the Navy were over. During my two years in Kingsville,

I had flown flights in the T-2C in all phases of student intermediate training (including Carrier Safety Pilot, Gunnery Instructor, Formation Instructor, and Uncontrolled Flight Instructor - Spins). I also flew in the TA-4J as Instrument Instructor, Night Familiarization Instructor, and Day Familiarization Instructor. In my career, I had accumulated over 3000 flight hours and 400 arrested landings (100 at night). My last flight in Kingsville and in the Navy was on June 3, 1991.

Time for Orders Again

After two years in Kingsville, it was two years to go until retirement. Time for orders. Normally for an officer's twilight tour (last assignment before retirement), he would be offered a nice billet. But my detailer offered me two billets I hated … for three reasons. First, they both involved significant at sea time away from my family; secondly, neither gave me an opportunity to fly; and thirdly, both billets were more administrative rather than operational. The billets offered to me were: Training Officer on *U.S.S. Enterprise* and Safety Officer on *U.S.S. Constellation*.

There was no way I was going to resign. I had to take some set of orders. Looking for alternatives, I asked the detailer if I could be assigned to the Naval Academy again, but he said there were no billets open there. The Department Chairman would have to accept me in some other billet and he probably wouldn't do that. So, I called the Mathematics Department Chairman just to see. He remembered me and said, "Sure, I think we can find something here for you." Two days later the detailer called me with orders for my twilight tour at the Naval Academy. What a wonderful way to end my Navy career!

CHAPTER 13

TWILIGHT YEARS

August 1991 – October 1993

Events in the Navy and Worldwide During This Time

May 22, 1992
> The Tonight Show Starring Johnny Carson aired its final show on NBC.

August 24 – August 28, 1992
> Hurricane Andrew hit south Florida. 23 were killed.

January 20, 1993
> Bill Clinton succeeded George H. W. Bush as the 42nd President of the United States.

March 13–March 15, 1993
> The Great Blizzard of 1993 stuck the eastern U.S., bringing record snowfall.

July 19, 1993
> U.S. President Bill Clinton announced his "Don't Ask, Don't Tell" policy regarding gays in the American military.

Naval Academy Housing

I had only two years to go for twenty years active service and retirement. In August 1991, the Herzog family made the trek from Texas to Annapolis. Within a few weeks, we had our housing assignment.

6 Longshaw Road - Our first house "on the yard" (on base United States Naval Academy). This house was long and narrow – kind of like Noah's Ark or a bowling alley. It had three bedrooms and a large kitchen for the six of us (soon to be seven). We stayed there for nearly a year. We really needed something bigger.

3 Wood Road – Our second house on the yard was much larger. Since we had five children, we rated a bigger house. This was one of the largest houses on the yard: second only to Buchanan House, the Superintendent's quarters. We called this house "The Mansion." It was bigger than any house we had ever lived in.

The Mansion

This house was built in 1910 and had four levels, nine bedrooms and five bathrooms. Can you imagine that? Each of our kids had their own bedroom on the third floor. I had a room for an office. Mary had a sewing room. There were still rooms left over. There was a huge unfinished basement with plenty of storage. This was truly a "cool" house.

Did I mention that the mansion was right next to the Naval Academy Hospital? It wasn't really a hospital, but everyone called it that. It was actually more like a clinic, but we could easily walk to it.

Children

Child #5 - Jennifer
"JJ"

March 7, 1990

Jennifer

Home Sweet Home

In September 1993, just prior to my retirement from the Navy, Mary and I purchased a house in Arnold, Maryland. It wasn't even built when we contracted to buy it. We got to watch it go up, from the foundation to the attic.

House #5
1503 Carrera Lane
Arnold, MD
September 1993

1503 Carrera Lane, Arnold

Naval Academy

By now I was a seasoned instructor. Actually, I was designated a Master Instructor, a title given to military instructors with significant experience. The civilian instructors all had doctorates and were designated "Professors." That title didn't apply to the military instructors unless, of course, they had their doctorates. I had previously taught all of the Mathematics core courses that the midshipmen were required to take. But during this tour of duty, I had the opportunity to teach some of the elective courses. Challenging and enjoyable.

At the end of a midshipman's second year, he (she) is required to sign a commitment to serve five years after graduation in "payment" for the two remaining years at the academy. This pledge is called "Two for Seven". They could resign from the academy and from Naval Service anytime during the first two years, with no financial obligation for their freshman and sophomore years, up to the time when they signed the commitment letter – The "Two for Seven."

Loyalties

During their first three years, Midshipmen were given glimpses of several Navy communities that they might serve in after graduation. They received some hands-on experience during their summer training and lots of advice and counsel through interaction with the officers assigned to the Naval Academy. The navy has a myriad of communities: Surface Navy, Naval Aviation, Submarines, Explosive Ordnance Disposal (EOD), Special Forces (Seals), Medical, Dental, Marine Ground, Marine Air, etc. As a senior officer at the Naval Academy, I had the opportunity to speak with a good number of midshipmen, in the classroom and socially. As these midshipmen entered their senior year, as "Firsties," they were given the opportunity to select which branch of the Navy they wanted to serve in for the five years of required service after graduation. At a designated date, they would submit a list of their prioritized choices for service. Then on a special night in the fall of their senior year, in the order of their class ranking, their service assignments would be announced. The first five years of their Navy journey as an officer was now mapped out.

Prior to their selection, when I spoke with these future officers, I often told them of my experiences and how the choice they would be making would affect their lives, just as mine did. Whatever their service assignment was, they would develop a loyalty to the other officers, men and women in that community. I used my own career as an example. Just like them, I could have become a Surface Warfare Officer, a Submariner, a Marine, a Seal, or a Naval Aviator, etc. I chose to be a Naval Aviator. To me, Naval Aviation was (and still is) the best.

Once in the Naval Aviation Training Pipeline, I could have chosen propeller aircraft, helos or jets. I choose jets. To me, jets were the best, but to the officers that choose props or helos, props or helos were the best. Within the jet pipeline, there were also choices: fighters, attack, anti-submarine warfare, electronic warfare, etc. I was assigned to be an Attack Pilot (a bomber pilot). To me, Attack was and still is the best.

Within the Attack community, there were several aircraft; A-7 Corsair II's, A-6 Intruders, A-4 Skyhawks, etc. I was assigned to fly A-7's. Of course, A-7's were the best. Within the A-7 community, there were numerous squadrons. I was assigned to Attack Squadron Nine Three (VA-93). VA-93 was the best. Get the idea?

I explained to these eager midshipmen that no matter which road they took, it would be the best in their eyes and their loyalty to the people who have traveled that road with them would be strong. So, they should make a choice that's best for them.

Army Week

One of the major events at the Naval Academy was the annual Army-Navy football game. The game itself is generally played in Philadelphia, New York, Baltimore, or some other neutral, military friendly site. At the Naval Academy, the week prior to the game is called "Army Week."

During Army Week, the midshipmen demonstrate their school spirit by performing various pranks, such as painting the Army mule blue and gold (Navy Colors) or shaving the Army mule's hair to say "N A V Y." But that kind of prank is left to a very few daring midshipmen, since it involves a trip to the West Point area and the very real possibility of being caught and perhaps having some unwanted mischief applied to them.

More commonly, the midshipmen looked for other opportunities at the Naval Academy. During Army Week, groups of them (groups consisting mainly of plebes, i.e. freshmen) would set out some time after midnight to do their well-planned mischief (Sometimes it was not so well-planned). There were three specific pranks that I remember having occurred during my eight years as an officer at the Naval Academy.

Prank #1: Mathematics Professors at the Naval Academy had their offices on the third floor of Chauvenet Hall. The offices were generally locked at night. One morning during Army Week, when a certain professor came to her office, she found a sign on the door. "BEAT ARMY --- ENTER AT YOUR OWN RISK."

When the professor unlocked and opened her door, thousands of packing "peanuts" poured out the door into the hallway. These annoying peanuts are small curly pieces of Styrofoam, used to keep breakable items safe when packed in a box. That unfortunate professor couldn't use her office for several hours that day.

No one knew where the pranksters got all of those peanuts, or how they got into the office, or how they got the peanuts to stay in the office so high against the door. The peanuts were piled at least five feet high. Midshipmen are very creative (and mischievous.)

Prank #2: The third floor Chauvenet Hall mathematics offices were accessible by stairs or elevator. One Army Week night, a group of midshipmen locked the doors at the top of the stairwell from the inside with chains and combination locks.

They all left the third floor by elevator. Then a group of them went back to the third floor on the elevator and somehow, propped a chair against the outside of the elevator doors and took the elevator to the basement. Then they sent the elevator back to the third floor. When the elevator doors opened on the third floor, the chair fell down in the door opening. When the doors started to close, they were prevented from closing by the obstructing chair and remained open. The elevator was essentially stuck on the third floor.

When the staff came to work in the morning, they had no way to get to their offices on the third floor. Eventually, Public Works was called and they sent a team so that the staff could regain access to the third floor of the building.

Prank #3: The next event occurred on a night that I was N.A.D.O. (Naval Academy Duty Officer). The N.A.D.O. was responsible for keeping an eye on things on the yard, while the rest of the staff was off duty. The watch generally started around 4 PM and lasted until about 8 AM the next morning.

The N.A.D.O. used a Navy sedan to get around and was allowed to go home if he lived in Navy Housing. Otherwise, he was expected to stay at the Bachelor Officer's Quarters (B.O.Q.) located above the Officer's Club.

On this particular night, I had made several trips around the yard. It was Army Week and I was on the lookout for mischievous activities. I had seen several small groups of midshipmen roaming around in various places, but none that were doing anything dangerous or illegal. At around 11 PM, I decided to go to the B.O.Q. to get some sleep.

Around 2 AM, I received a call from the Naval Academy Police Department about a blockage of the College Creek Bridge. I was needed to resolve the situation. The College Creek Bridge was on the yard and connected the housing areas with the main campus.

When I got to the bridge, I found an A-4 Skyhawk (a jet aircraft) in the middle of the bridge. This display aircraft was generally on a pedestal near the fire station in the housing area. I was told by a policeman that midshipmen had taken it off of its pedestal and moved it to its present location. They were planning to take it to Buchanan House which is where the Naval Academy Superintendent lived. The Superintendent was a vice admiral who served as the university president. Obviously, the midshipmen were discovered and their plan was foiled. However, now there was an airplane on the bridge, in the middle of the road.

In case you are wondering how the aircraft was returned to its proper position, I called Bancroft Hall (midshipmen dormitory) and spoke with the "Firstie" (first class midshipman – a senior) on duty. I told him to get a crew of midshipmen over to the College Creek Bridge to return the A-4 to its pedestal. These midshipmen would quite likely include many of the same ones who moved the airplane to its present position. Within 90 minutes the aircraft was back where it belonged and things were more or less back to normal.

Retirement

As my two-year assignment at the Naval Academy was nearing an end, so was my career with the Navy. On October 1, 1993, I retired from active duty. When a Naval Officer retires, he traditionally has a retirement ceremony. This is a formal affair, where his superiors and peers come together to review and speak about his career. I was honored to have my two supervising officers come to speak at my retirement: Captain Kendall and Commander Kroshl. I was given an opportunity to speak as well. Generally, the retiring officer is given the opportunity to reflect upon his twenty years and leave his audience with a few words of wisdom from his experiences in the Navy.

I was impressed and honored that so many people came to see me off. I wasn't sure whether they were truly honoring me or were just happy to see me go. At a designated time, during the ceremony, I was "piped over the side with honors." A boatswain's mate blew his boatswain pipe (whistle) and the

Commander Marty Herzog and Mary -- piped over the side

announcement "Commander Martin Herzog, departing," was made. As the band played, Mary and I walked through the lines of side boys, while I returned their salute. Then it was over. I was wished "Fair Winds and Following Seas," a popular Navy expression when someone is leaving or retiring.

My career was over, but my life in the Navy was not. When an officer retires, he is still considered an officer and is addressed by his rank. I was still Commander Herzog. I was once again unemployed, but it felt good to have successfully completed my career in the Navy.

POST RETIREMENT

October 1993 – January 2018

In October 1993, after twenty-six years in the Navy (twenty years active duty), I retired. At the age of 47, I wasn't ready to really retire, so I began looking for a job to begin my second career. Actually, I began looking well before October, and I wasn't having much success.

Due to my years of educational experience, I thought I would have an easy time finding a job in a community college. The college in Anne Arundel County (my home county) had no positions open, so I expanded my search. I looked in Maryland, Virginia, Delaware as well as … can you believe it? … Tennessee. I had several interviews, but no serious job offers. Obviously, I was very disappointed.

Eventually Mary and I decided to commit to stay in Maryland and in our local church, trusting God to lead me to a suitable job without having to move. Then, we told our pastor of this commitment. He seemed pleased but concerned that I couldn't find employment. The very next week, I received a phone call from Don Berkowitz, (Math and Science Division Chairman at Chesapeake College in Wye Mills, Maryland), asking me if I would be interested in interviewing for a position at Chesapeake College.

Chesapeake College

I interviewed and was hired on the spot. I was to be the Computer Science Department Chairman. In this position, I was actually overseeing several other small departments as well. I had not submitted a job application or resume to Chesapeake College. I have no idea how Dr. Berkowitz knew me or how he knew I was looking for a job, but there I was, gainfully employed once again.

I had majored in Computer Science for my masters degree from Johns Hopkins University and it seemed obvious that Chesapeake College was more interested in my Computer Science background than my Mathematics experience. So instead of teaching math, as I had been doing at the Naval Academy for eight years, I was now teaching Computer Science, which was a great change of pace for me, but I really enjoyed it.

Daily commuting to Chesapeake involved a round trip of about 60 miles (thirty each way) and two trips over the Chesapeake Bay Bridge during rush hour. But – not so bad – since the morning rush hour traffic was mostly heading west while I was heading east and the evening rush hour traffic – just the opposite. So, my daily commute was pretty easy and took about half an hour each way.

New Covenant Church

After three years at Chesapeake College, I was offered a job at my church, New Covenant Church in Arnold, Maryland. In August 1996 I began a new and very different employment path, as Church Administrator, Financial Manager and Worship Leader. I served in this capacity for 12 years.

During this period, the elders and congregation decided to construct a new building on a different site, about

New Covenant Church

a mile away from the previous building, on the corner of Jones Station Road and College Parkway.

It took several years to design and build this facility at a cost of $2.3 million. In June 2001, it was finally complete, and we moved in.

During my twelve years as New Covenant Church Administrator, I was able to return to the United States Naval Academy to work part time, teaching mathematics for three semesters (during 2003, 2007 and 2008). It was great to be working with midshipmen again.

Fire!

In January 2002, two of my daughters (ages 18 and 15) were home alone and one of them decided to make some candles. She put paraffin in a pot on the stove to melt and left the kitchen with the pot unattended (mistake number one). Before long the paraffin reached its flash point and the liquid caught fire. The wax was still contained in the pot, but it was blazing away. Upon returning to the kitchen, my daughter found the pot boiling with flames reaching up several inches above the rim of the pot. Panicking, she got a glass of water and threw it on the burning wax (mistake number two). The burning paraffin splattered onto the stove and the wall behind the stove catching it on fire as well. Before long the wall was engulfed with flames. One of the girls called 911 to report the fire. They were told to immediately leave the house.

The fire department responded quickly and put out the fire. However, the kitchen was a total loss and the ceilings in the house were completely black due to the smoke. The kitchen floor and basement floor were covered with water from the fire hoses.

Estimated $25,000 damage. That night, we moved into Embassy Suites

Fire damage

and stayed there for six weeks while repairs to our house were made.

There was a bit of good news:

1) This damage and the hotel bill were paid for by insurance.
2) Mary got to pick all new cabinets and kitchen appliances.
3) We replaced the damaged carpets and linoleum with wood flooring throughout the house.

So, our house got a face-lift.

Our daughters were instructed by the fire department personnel that the correct way to put out the fire would have been to put the cover over the pot, thereby smothering it by depriving the fire of needed oxygen.

Déjà vu

As an eleven-year-old boy, I loved to make camp fires. I was a boy scout and learned to make fires for camping and cooking. I enjoyed the challenge making a fire from scratch, finding the wood, kindling, twigs and branches, and then getting it going so that I could use it to cook a meal. I think most 11 or 12-year-old boys enjoy making fires.

I remember one day in 1957, my friend Scott and I were playing behind a small barn (about the size of a six-car garage with two levels) in my backyard – about 100 feet from the back door of our house. We were playing with matches, making a fire (but really, we were playing with matches). We couldn't get the fire going with the wood that we had. I noticed some insulation (straw) protruding from the barn roof. Wondering if this would help, I tried to light it with my matches. No luck.

Soon, we gave up on fire-making and moved on to other entertainment.

A short time later, Scott had to go home. After he left, I went behind the barn to collect the match residue and any tell- tale wood scraps. I didn't want to get caught in my sin. When I reached the site, to my horror I discovered that the straw actually did catch fire and the barn was burning. Now what? Quick thinker that I am, I raced to the house, found a pitcher in the kitchen, filled it with water from the sink and raced back to the barn and threw the water onto the fire – no effect. The wall of the barn was still burning.

So, back to the house for another pitcher full of water and back to the barn again. Still no change. Actually, the fire looked to be spreading. Back to the house for another pitcher. What else could I do? My mom, who was in the kitchen watching my sprints to and from the barn with pitchers of water, got a bit curious and followed me out to the barn and discovered the fire. She called the fire department (no 911 in those days).

Two fire trucks came and put out the blaze. Meanwhile, I ran into my bedroom and hid under my bed, hoping that everyone would forget that I was the one who caused this problem. However, my "trial" and punishment would come later.

My father, who had no idea of what was transpiring, was on the way home from a hard day at work. When he turned down the street to our house, he saw the fire trucks and hoses strewn across the street. and thought to himself, "Some poor son-of-a-gun had a fire." As he neared our house, he realized that he was that son-of-a-gun. And he soon found out that his oldest son was responsible.

Now, back to year 2002. While I was at work on that fateful candle-making day, I received a call from one of my daughters as they were standing outside of our home, while the fire department was hosing down our kitchen. She said that our house was on fire and that I had better come home. Now 45 years after I set the barn on fire, I was the father coming home to find fire trucks and hoses at my house. As they say, "What goes around, comes around."

Cars

During these years from 1993 to 2018, we owned six more cars. As of 2018, we still have the Yukon, Chrysler and the Corolla. It seems like we always have three or four cars parked in our driveway.

Car #15 1993 Blue Chevy Astro 11/97

Car #16 1997 Red Chevy Blazer

Car #17 2001 Blue Saturn LW300 wagon

Car #18 2001 Pewter Yukon GMC

Car #19 2008 Silver Chrysler Town and Country 1/2010

Car #20 2011 Grey Toyota Corolla

2001 Blue Saturn
(Justin on skateboard)

Herzog "Parking Lot"

The Yukon is mine. The grey Corolla is Mary's. The Chrysler is a wheel chair conversion van that is MaLisa's. Now Jennifer has a Corolla as well. So, there are four cars in our driveway every night.

U.S. Naval Academy (ten more years)

In the years after the turn of the century, New Covenant Church leadership was experiencing some internal strife, causing some of the congregation to leave. As a result, the church finances began to falter. Due to the strife and the failing finances of the church, I began to look for different employment.

In August 2008, after 12 years as Administrator of New Covenant Church, I was hired by the Naval Academy's Academic Center as a Mathematics Learning Specialist. This full-time position involved working with the midshipmen who were struggling with math or just wanted to do better than they were. I also taught one section of Youngster (Sophomore) math with the Mathematics Department each semester.

Then on December 31, 2018, after ten more years at the Naval Academy, I retired from full time federal service.

Looking back through the many years in the Navy and serving the Navy, I can say, "It's been good."

Family

Left to right: Marty, Maryel, MaLisa, Jennifer, Mary, Elizabeth, Kevin

A Grandson

Grandson #1:
Justin Mathew Herzog
September 12, 2003

Justin

*Jennifer's expression says it all.
It's been a great ride.*

REMEMBERING

This is a list of many of the men who died during or after the time that I served with them. I may have missed some names and I may have some incorrect information but these errors are purely unintentional. It does not minimize the level of honor to which these men are due. I have listed them by order of their dates of death.

These are men that served our nation well.

---

21 March 1969   Ed Herdrich
                                 Student Naval Aviator and friend

Killed while in the landing pattern at night at NAS Chase Field, Beeville, Texas

---

5 February 1970

Rick Stephenson

Naval Aviator - VA-93 (USS Ranger) Lost at sea shortly after night launch

A-7B Corsair II

---

18 March 1971

Bob "Skip" Graff

Naval Aviator and roommate, Naval Academy graduate.

Crashed in A7-E - Night Bombing Practice in California

---

19 October 1971

LCDR K L Rasmussen
LT N.J. Tucker
LT D.H. Vonpritchyns
LT E.B. Pearlman
AT2 Roger Poe

VAW-115 E2 midair collision with A-7

---

23 May 1972   Charlie Barnett

                                     Naval Aviator – XO VA-93 (USS
                                     Midway)

Assigned to VA-93 as XO scheduled to eventually become Commanding
Officer. Believed to have been shot down by a SAM

---

19 July 1972   Donnelly Raymond P

                                     A6 VA-115

---

23 July 1972   Gary L Shank

                                     A7 VA-56 MIA

Shot down southwest of Haiphong. Photos of his helmet and parts of
his aircraft appeared in print, but he was never recovered or heard from.

---

8 August 1972   LCDR James L Anderson
                                     AZ1 Bobby Don Cobb

                                     E-2 VAW 115

---

25 Aug 1972   Michael W Doyle

                               F-4 VF 151 MIA

---

7 September 1972   Don A Gerstell

                              Naval   Aviator   VA-93   (USS
                              Midway)

On a surveilance mission over Hon Nieu, North Vietnam, his aircraft was struck by lightning. He crashed midway between Hon Nieu and Hon Matt. His remains were not recovered.

---

24 October 1972   LTJG Michael S Bixell   A-6 VA115
                  AMSAN Daniel P Cherry   VA-93
                  AA Robert W Haakenson, Jr   V-1 Div
                  AA Robert A Yankoski   V-4 Div
                  AO2 Clayton M Blankenship   VA-56

An A-6 Intruder returning from a night combat mission over North Vietnam at close to maximum carrier landing weight with two 500 pound bombs hung on its right outboard weapons station, landed successfully. However the right axle sheared off on contact with the flight deck. The aircraft tailhook disengaged from the arresting gear wire and the A-6 slid up the flight deck into parked aircraft.

---

6 November 1972   Clarence O "Smokey" Tolbert

A-7 VA56 MIA
Blue Angel #6, 1968

Shot down and lost over North Vietnam. Believed to have been shot down while on a low-level photo reconnaissance mission over the Vinh River.

---

6 January 1973   John Lindahl

A7 VA-56

His A-7 veered and dove into the ocean shortly after takeoff. The crash was observed from the ship, and within 45 seconds, helicopters and divers were on the scene, but his body was never recovered

---

10 January 1973   LT Michael McCormick
                                  LT(jg) Robert Clark

A-6 VA-115 MIA

Arab 511 was on a SAM and Radar Suppression mission in support of B-52's on a *Linebacker II* operation. After going "feet dry", they were never heard from again.

---

3 April 1973

Gary Simpkins

Naval Aviator - VA-93 (USS Ranger)

VA22 USS Coral Sea - Lost at Sea
His plane had just launched off the USS Coral Sea when it lost power and plunged into sea.

---

12 November 1973

Richard "Sparky" Pierson

Returning to Japan from Korea in instrument conditions, when the controller cleared him to "one five thousand". He responded on the radio "descending to five thousand" and later hit a 5200-foot hill right at 5000 feet.

---

9 January 1980

Gaylord Parrett

Naval Aviator VA-93 (USS Ranger)

Lost at sea Near San Clemente, CA

---

12 November 1980   Pete Leum

                                    Naval Aviator and roommate
                                    (1969)

lost his life when his VX-5 TA-7C Corsair II crashed while simulating
close air support at Ft. Irwin.

---

12 September 2001   Dave Glunt

                                    Naval Aviator
                                    Commanding Officer VA-93
                                    (10/69 – 6/70)

---

28 January 2006   Carl "Dad" Erie

   Naval Aviator
                                    Commanding Officer VA-93
                                    (7/71 – 7/72)

---

10 November 2009   Rudy Kohn

Naval Aviator
Commanding Officer VA-93
(11/70 – 7/71)

---

25 December 2011   Greg Wren

Naval Aviator VA-93 (USS Midway)

His best story from the war years was about meeting the actor John Wayne over the chess board while on carrier duty. After losing the match, the "Duke" did a classic double take: "Well, I enjoyed it," exiting the cabin and then sticking his head back in under the hatchway, he said, "The hell I did!"

---

2 August 2012   Marv Reynolds

Naval Aviator
X.O. VA-174 (1969)

---

20 November 2015   "Mugs" McKeown

Mugs, along with his R.I.O., Jack Ensch shot down two MIG-17s on a single combat Air Patrol north of Hanoi. Both were awarded the Navy Cross

First Commanding Officer of TOPGUN.

Printed in the United States
By Bookmasters